OSPREY
MILITARY

ELITE SERIES | 37

PANAMA 1989-90

Text by
GORDON ROTTMAN
Colour plates by
RON VOLSTAD

D1567363

British Library Cataloguing in Publication Data

Rottman, Gordon L.
Panama 1989–90. —(Elite)
I. Title   II. Series
972.8703
ISBN 1855321564

Filmset in Great Britain
Printed through Bookbuilders Ltd, Hong Kong

Acknowledgements

Operation 'Just Cause' was an extremely involved
operation, undoubtedly the most complex of this scale
(until Operation 'Desert Shield') undertaken by US
armed forces since Vietnam. This book would not have
been possible without the assistance and advice of
many closely involved with the operation and those
who assisted by providing additional information. The
author sincerely thanks Ken Atkins, Geoffrey T.
Barker (US Spl. Opns. Cmd.), Bob Bockman
(Audiovisual Media Support, Asst. Secretary of
Defense), Reyola H. Carlisle (Public Affairs Office, Ft.
Ord), Robert T. Cates (Lt. Col. USAF Ret.), Maj.
Brian A. Kilgariff (JRTC), Maj. Bill Lindley (75th
Ranger Regt.), Maj. Charles D. Melson (USMC
Historical Center), Capt. Wayne D. Perry (24th
Composite Wing), and Col. George H. Stinnett
(Policy & Plans Div., Secretary of the Army). A very
special thanks goes to Capt. David Hoagey and the
really great bunch of guys of the Air Force's Det. 5,
602nd Tactical Air Control Wing (attached to the 7th
Inf. Div.). I would also like to thank my wife
Enriqueta for handling the Spanish translations.

Note:

The author has attempted to describe accurately the
deployment and movements of the many units
committed to Operation 'Just Cause'. Unfortunately,
official records have not yet been declassified and many
of the available open sources contain conflicting dates
and unit movements. Additionally, the XVIII Abn.
Corps and 82d Abn. Div. were unavailable as an
information source due to their deployment to Saudi
Arabia in support of Operation 'Desert Shield'.
Regrettably, a complete listing of the US order of
battle was not available.

INTRODUCTION

Combat actions by a democratic free world force must satisfy the operational principles of feasibility, suitability, and acceptability. In a democracy the decision to use force can never be an easy choice. It must be feasible: that is, it must be within the capabilities of the force and possess a high probability of achieving success. Just as importantly, the decision must be suitable and appropriate, meaning the force will accomplish its mission in support of national and free world interests. Finally, the decision must be acceptable in that the desired results are worth the costs ... and risks.

Military responses today are also governed by three key legal principles; they must be justified, proportionate, and discriminate. Justification requires a country to act in self-defense not only of its sovereign territory but of its interests and citizens abroad, or, in appropriate instances, in aid of others incapable of protecting themselves from aggression or oppression. Proportionality requires that a military response be consistent with the hostile act and/or that it be sufficient to counter the threat without resulting in undue escalation or in more than the minimum necessary interference with other states. The principle of discrimination requires that the response be directed only at those responsible for the commission of the hostile acts. Reasonable precautions must be taken to limit civilian casualties and reduce collateral damage.

In late 1989, while much of Eastern Europe was beginning to realize its own new-found freedom, the United States found itself enmeshed in a progressively trying situation with the belligerent and illegal government of a country with which it has long had friendly, though unfortunately sometimes stormy, relations and with which it is deeply involved economically. Though the term 'tragic' is over-used today and may even seem trite, Operation 'Just Cause' was indeed a tragic development and should never have taken place, though it was due to circumstances long out of control. To analyze those causes is not the goal of this book; it will briefly discuss those causes, but will focus principally on the military aspects of Operation 'Just Cause' and the actions of the committed armed forces units. It is the story of the men and women who successfully executed an extremely complex operation under difficult circumstances.

PANAMA AND THE USA

The United States' direct interest in Panama—then a province of Colombia—began in the 1840s and 1850s; a treaty was concluded giving the US transit rights across the isthmus, and a US-built railway was completed in 1855. Many pioneers bound for California and Oregon travelled across Panama rather than endure the long voyage round Cape Horn. Early interest in digging a canal faded when the Transcontinental Railroad spanned America in 1869. In the 1880s Ferdinand de Lesseps, mastermind of the Suez Canal, was defeated in his attempts to build a canal across the isthmus. US government interest in such a project was rekindled by the needs of the military during the Spanish-American War of 1898.

Negotiations in 1903 aimed at securing US control of a strip of territory and the right to build a canal failed. The US undoubtedly had some involvement in the subsequent revolt by Panama against Colombian rule in November that year, whose success was largely guaranteed by Colombia's weakness due to a bloody civil war in 1899–1902. The Republic of Panama was recognized by the USA on 6 Nov. 1903, and two weeks later a treaty was ratified. The Hay-Bunau-Varilla Treaty granted the US possession of a ten-mile strip across the isthmus, coastal positions for the defense of the future canal, water reservoir and support sites, and partial control of Panama City on the Pacific side and Colon on the Caribbean, these being the projected termini. In return the US paid a cash sum and agreed annuities.

Construction of the Panama Canal—the most massive construction project since the Great Wall of China—was undertaken between 1907 and 1915, the first ship actually passing through on 15 Aug. 1914. The Panama Canal Zone was a US possession, under a governor appointed by Congress; Panama itself was a US protectorate, eventually recognized by Colombia in 1921.

The Canal has remained the central feature of Panamanian economic development. It provides direct and indirect employment for many thousands of Panamanians, and the urban population enjoys a relatively higher standard of living than those of other regional countries. The magnet to all kinds of international commerce represented by the Canal, and by Panama's relaxed corporate regulations, has drawn in many foreign-owned companies and banks. US currency is the official medium of exchange throughout the Republic. (Despite these advantages, the excesses of the Noriega regime have left Panama with massive foreign debts and suffering under severe World Bank restrictions.) In such a *laissez faire* environment it is hardly surprising that until the 1970s Panama's rulers were drawn from a select group of businessmen whose interests were closely attuned to those of the USA; some observers have described Panama's government as functioning largely as an international corporation rather than a bureaucratic administration.

The country's dependence on the US has often been resented by citizens who regard the US connection as a 'colonial presence'. Panama's domestic situation was usually tranquil, but there were occasions of internal strife, usually in the form of riots and strikes protesting Panamanian government policies. Little of this was directed against the Canal Zone's US government, which was generally viewed as a permanent fixture and a necessity. However, when the Panamanian National Guard (the armed forces) and police were unable to cope with the situation, US troops from the Canal defense forces were requested by the Panamanian government to intervene on numerous occasions in 1917–18, the 1920s and early 1930s. In 1931 the US granted

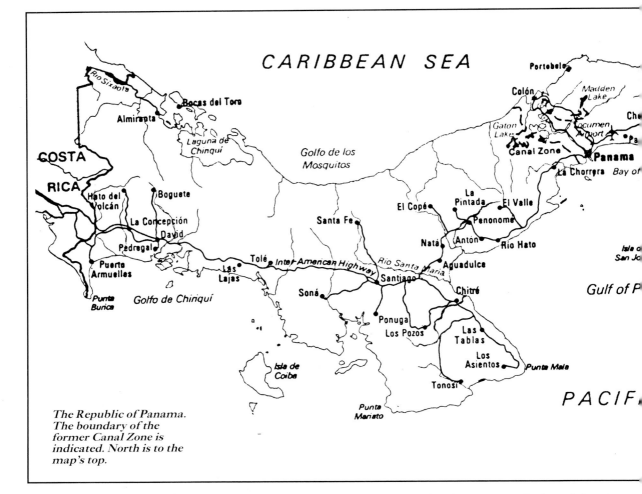

The Republic of Panama.
The boundary of the
former Canal Zone is
indicated. North is to the
map's top.

Panama a higher degree of self-determination and thereafter would no longer intervene militarily in Panamanian politics. A strong form of Panamanian nationalism, *Panameñismo*, began to develop through the 1940s and 1950s. In early 1959 the playboy son of a former Panamanian president led a small band of Cuban adventurers in a comic opera invasion (not supported by Castro); landing on the north coast, they were promptly rounded up by the National Guard. The rural land reform protests in the early and mid-1960s were also dealt with by the Panamanians themselves.

For over 40 years the dominant opposition leader in Panama was one Arnulfo Arias. Twice elected in the 1940s, he was twice defeated in subsequent elections. In 1964 vicious rioting broke out in protest at the US presence, the most serious to date; four US soldiers and 24 Panamanians lost their lives. Though urged to confront the US military by the rioting factions, the National Guard wisely refrained from entering the fray. In 1968 Arnulfo Arias was again elected, but was ousted in less than two weeks, and a military junta gained control of the country. The following year Col. Omar Torrijos gained complete power. All political parties were abolished, and he administered the country through a series of puppet civilian governments. Torrijos, the 'Maximum Chief', dominated Panamanian politics and increased his small country's regional influence. To instill a stronger sense of

nationalism Torrijos became outspokenly anti-American an befriended Castro's Cuba. Many feel that Torrijos was simp 'playing both ends' in order to achieve the best advantage fe Panama. He never threatened to terminate the extensive financi relations with the US, nor protested the presence of US arme forces in the Canal Zone (viewed by some Panamanians as a ba for US regional expansionism), nor called for the ejection of tl US from the Canal Zone other than by the due process of tl 1979 treaty with the Carter Administration. Torrijos permitte the re-establishment of political parties and presidential electio in 1978, a preliminary requirement of the treaty.

Torrijos' major contribution to Panama's future was tl controversial Carter-Torrijos Treaty of 1978, signed on 1 Oc 1979. In an action strongly opposed by US conservative President Jimmy Carter's administration developed a treaty th will turn over total control of the Canal to Panama on 31 De 1999. The Canal Zone ceased to exist as such with the signing the treaty, and the territory returned to Panamanian authorit though the US still retains complete right of access to the are The Canal itself is now jointly managed by the US and Panam US armed forces will be withdrawn by New Year's Day in th year 2000, though the treaty provides for ten years of US milita assistance to insure the Canal's security. Until then, the Carte Torrijos Treaty permits the US to intervene militarily to prote

ir

Río Chepo

del Rey

La Palma

Río Tuira

EAN

COLOMBIA

Notes on US Army designation practices

(1) Troops and batteries are company-size. Squadrons are battalion-size. Detachments are generally platoon or smaller size, but function administratively as a company.
(2) Combat arms battalions can only be identified by the inclusion of their parent regiment's designation, which provides only a traditional designation. Regimental headquarters are not assigned to tactical formations and have no tactical control over units (with the exception of the 75th Ranger Regt., non-divisional armored cavalry regiments, and SF battalions which are assigned to groups).
(3) Airborne infantry battalions assigned to the 82nd Abn. Div. have parent regiments designated either Parachute Infantry or Airborne Infantry for traditional reasons.
(4) Infantry battalions and their organic companies are designated, e.g. Co. A, 1st Bn., 509th Inf. For brevity's sake, this will appear as A/1-508. The hyphen signifies the traditional linkage of the battalion with the parent regiment. Rangers and SF are shown A/2/75 Rangers and C/3/7 SF since their regimental/group headquarters do have tactical control. Non-infantry combat arms units will have their designation followed by their branch (ADA, Armor, Avn., Cav., FA).
(5) Three to five maneuver battalions may be attached to a brigade and are not permanently assigned since they can be switched between brigades and even divisions. Brigades may be organic to a division or separate.

Abbreviations

Units

Plt	Platoon
Det	Detachment
Co	Company
Bty	Battery
Trp	Troop
Bn	Battalion
Sdn	Squadron
Bde	Brigade
Grp	Group
Regt	Regiment
Div	Division

Branches/Misc

Abn	Airborne	MI	Military Intelligence
ADA	Air Defense Artillery	MP	Military Police
AFB	Air Force Base	Psyops	Psychological Operations
Armd	Armored		
ARNG	Army National Guard	SEAL	Sea-Air-Land
Avn	Aviation	Sep	Separate
CA	Civil Affairs	SF	Special Forces
FA	Field Artillery	SFGA	Special Forces Group (Abn)
Inf	Infantry		
JTFSO	Joint Task Force South	Spt	Support
		TF	Task Force
JOTC	Jungle Operations Training Center	Trans	Transportation
		USAF	US Air Force
Lt	Light	USAR	US Army Reserve
Maint	Maintenance	USMC	US Marine Corps
Mech	Mechanized	USN	US Navy

he Canal and other US interests. Whether it will prove a serious miscalculation for the US to relinquish control of such an economically and militarily strategic asset in a region known for political and economic instability, and whether Panama can effectively operate and responsibly manage the related economic spin-offs, remains to be seen.

Gen. Torrijos' death in a helicopter crash in 1981 heralded a new and more turbulent era. Between 1982 and 1985 Panama endured five new presidents, most of whom were ineffective, and all of whom were forced to resign. During this period of turmoil a new commander-in-chief of the National Defense Forces was appointed by Col. Ruben Dario Paredes, the then commander-

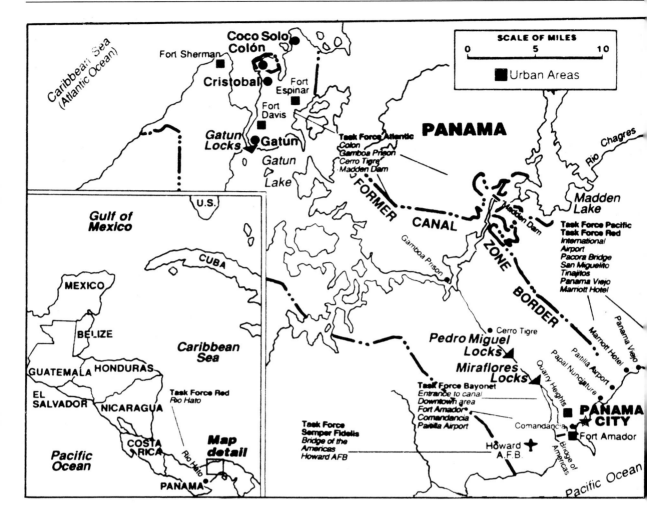

The former Canal Zone and environs indicating key locations and the approximate areas of operations for Task Forces Atlantic, Bayonet, Pacific, Red, and Semper Fidelis.

in-chief, who resigned in order to run for the presidency. This was Col. Manuel Antonio Noriega, the former G-2, who later convinced Paredes to withdraw from the race. By 1985 Eric Arturo Devalle, the former vice-president, was instated as the new president, but under Panama's peculiar brand of democracy the defense forces' commander-in-chief actually controls the reins of power.

It was not long before Noriega was in complete control of the government, with the president and legislative assembly being mere figureheads and administrators. Noriega and his defense forces cronies were soon deeply involved in all sorts of shady dealings ranging from kickbacks from government agencies and Canal related businesses to gun running, drug trafficking, and exchanging US generated intelligence with the Cubans ... and vice versa. He was implicated in the murder of a popular Torrijos aide believed to be preparing an exposé of Noriega's abuses. Open criticism of Noriega began in the US press in mid-1986, and abrasive accusations were exchanged between the US and

Panamanian governments. Relations began to deteriorate rapidly; and by the end of 1987 the Panamanian government threatened to suspend the visas of US Southern Command personnel, ejected all US Agency for International Development personnel from the country, and cancelled the annual combined Canal defense exercise. (Since the 1979 Sandinista takeover of Nicaragua the US Southern Command, with operational control of US armed forces' activities throughout Latin America, served as a target for the protests of Communist and leftist factions and a scapegoat to be blamed for the region's troubles.) Noriega by no means enjoyed the popular support of the majority of his nation's citizens. Demanding his resignation, riots and strikes broke out in protest at his flagrant abuses. The rift between the US and Noriega continued to grow, and events careered rapidly out of control.

The land and the people

We will digress briefly to summarize geographic and demographic points as they affect this book. Occupying the south-eastern end of the Central American land bridge connecting North and South Americas, Panama is bordered by a passive Costa Rica to the north-west, and to the south-east by Colombia, with which Panama has developed close economic and military ties, and by Venezuela. While the Canal is thought of as connecting the eastern Caribbean Sea, the 'Atlantic side', and the western Pacific, Panama's long axis is actually east to west and the Canal runs north-west to south-east. Panama itself appears somewhat like a flattened 'S' on its side. The capital, Panama City (pop. 455,000), is just to the north-east of the port of Balboa at the Canal's terminus. The Greater Panama City area, however, stretching north-east from the Canal, has a total population of about a million. The second largest city, Colón (87,000), shares the Canal's northern terminus with the port of Cristóbal. Over 40,000 non-military American citizens live in Panama.

A number of US military bases dot the former Canal Zone and include, on the Pacific end, west of the Canal: Ft. Knobbe, Howard AFB, and Rodman Naval Air Station. In and around Panama City east of the Canal are the interlinked Forts Amador and Grant (turned over to the Panamanians, though Amador is a shared base), Albrook AFB north of Panama City, Ft. Clayton to the north of Albrook, and Quarry Heights within Panama City (housing the US Southern Command headquarters). On the Caribbean side and west of the Canal is Ft. Sherman, location of the Army's Jungle Operations Training Center (JOTC), and to the south of it Pena Firing Range. On the east side Forts Randolph, Gulick and William F. Davis are positioned around Colón. Some US military posts, such as Forts Amador, Grant and Cimarrón, had been turned over to Panamanian forces in 1980 under the provisions of the Carter-Torrijos Treaty.

The majority of the country consists of low mountains and hills covered by light evergreen forests and scrub in the western provinces and extremely dense tropical jungles in the east. Panama covers about the same area as South Carolina. Two mountain ranges form the isthmus' backbone with a conveniently low section at the second narrowest point where the Canal was constructed. The Caribbean side has a much higher rainfall than the Pacific side, which also has a more defined dry season. The jungles and mountains in the country's eastern half are the most rugged in Central America; the Inter-American Highway, running from Alaska down through South America, is broken only in inhospitable eastern Panama, with no plans to complete the project in the foreseeable future. A bridge did not span the Canal itself until after World War II, but several now do. In December and January, the period of 'Just Cause', the day temperatures were in the 90s F with equally high humidity.

The culture and customs of the people are Caribbean Spanish, the majority being of mixed Spanish and Indian (Mestizo or Cholo) descent. The predominant minorities are indigenous Indians and West Indians. Total population is approximately 2,275,000. Spanish is the official language with approximately 14 per cent of the population speaking English (virtually a second official language), especially West Indians, businessmen, professionals, and most of those employed by the Panama Canal Commission. Panama has a high literacy rate for the region: 62

Gen. Manuel Noriega (second right) is briefed on an exercise by PDF officers wearing uniforms almost identical to the US lightweight Battle Dress Uniform (BDU). (From a Noriega photo album via Capt. D. Hoagey)

per cent in rural and 94 per cent in urban areas. The bulk of the population is concentrated in the urban centers at both ends of the Canal, while most of the rural population resides in the western provinces. As was demonstrated during and after 'Just Cause', the vast majority of the people are pro-American.

Panama's administrative subdivisions include nine provinces (*provincias*) and the Administration (*intendencia*) of San Blas, a rugged strip on the north-east coast populated only by a few Indians.

PANAMANIAN DEFENSE FORCES

Panama's first attempt at a national army was short lived; it attempted a coup soon after the country achieved independence, and in the consequent anti-military mood a National Police (*Policía Nacional*) was formed in its place. From 1904 to 1953 the National Police's principal rôle was solely that of law enforcement and internal security, and it refrained from any serious political involvement. Even during World War II the National Police was not significantly integrated into US Canal defense plans. Panama was one of two Latin American countries (the other being Argentina, considered somewhat pro-Nazi) that did not receive Lend-Lease aid from the US; Roosevelt did not want large quantities of arms provided to an, even then, troublesome National Police.

In 1953 the police were transformed into a paramilitary force, the National Guard (*Guardia Nacional*); still responsible for police functions, the new force was additionally tasked with some traditionally military missions. This also opened a new era (1953–83) of political interference, with the National Guard often acting as an arbiter of political power. The early and mid-1960s saw the National Guard involved in countering student riots and a small rural guerrilla movement. In 1968 Col. Omar Torrijos Herrera seized power in a coup and from then on the National Guard was *the* political power in the Panamanian government. Though it was trained and equipped by the US, some military assistance was received from Venezuela; and Torrijist officers tended to be more outspoken against the US than their own politicians. In 1979 the National Guard began to assume an even more military rôle as stipulated by the Carter-Torrijos Treaty. Destined eventually to take resonsibility for the Canal's defense, a number of conventional and specialized Infantry Companies were formed. In 1984, the year after Gen. Manuel Antonio Noriega gained power, the National Guard was redesignated the Defense Forces of Panama (*Fuerzas de Defensa de Panamá*), more commonly known as the Panamanian Defense Forces (PDF). Hereafter the dates of unit/organization formation are given in parentheses.

Comprising four branches, the PDF's main headquarters was located at *La Comandancía* in the south part of Panama City. A few miles away is the small Patilla Airport where Noriega kept several aircraft. The Ground Force (*Fuerza Terrestre*) was composed of over 6,000 personnel. The force was divided into 12 military zones (*Ciudad de Panamá* and 2–12° *Zona Militar*), commanders of some having substantial power due to their

loyalty to Noriega. Some military zones had one or more named Reaction Platoons (*Pelotón de Reacción*), intended to back the police.

The PDF was headed by the Defense Forces commander-in-chief, Manuel Noriega; the president was the purely nominal commander-in-chief, and there was no separate minister of defense. Key agencies included the General Staff (G-1 through 5), various special staffs, Adjutant General, Defense and Security Commission, and Special Forces Operational Command (*Comando Operacional de Fuerzas Especiales*—1985)[1]. Since 1987 the real control of the PDF was not exercised by the General Staff but rather by the Strategic Military Council (*Consjo Estrategico Militar*), a collection of roughly 12 of Noriega's most trusted cronies ranging in grade from captain to colonel—in the PDF an individual's rank was not always indicative of the authority he held. Handpicked by Noriega for their loyalty and abilities, *La Consjo* made major policy decisions and plans subject to Noriega's approval, and initiated any actions needed to maintain Noriega in power, often overriding the General Staff; there was a simmering resentment between the two bodies. Noriega also directly oversaw the Ground Forces while the other services were directed by the Chiefs of the Air, Naval, and Police Forces, all answering to Noriega.

Though conscription was authorized by law, the PDF relied solely on volunteers. PDF enlisted personnel received three months' basic training. The PDF's Military Institute at Rio Hato Military Base[2] conducted officer cadet training plus some low-level officer courses. Most advanced officer training was undertaken in Chile, Colombia, El Salvador, Mexico, Venezuela, and the USA. Advisors were also provided by Cuba and Nicaragua. The PDF maintained a number of service schools:

Military Institute (*Instituto Militar 'Gen Tomás Herrera'*—1974)—Rio Hato
NCO School (*Escuela de Suboficiales 'Gen. Benjamín Ruíz'*—1986)—Rio Hato
Military Instruction Center (*Centro de Instruccion Militar 'Cimarrón'*—1969)—La Joya
Military Skills Center (*Centro de Adiestraniento Militar 'Gen. José Domingo Espinar'*—1984)—Ft. Espinar
Female Formation School (*Escuela de Formacion Femenina 'Rufina Alfaro'*—1985)—Gamboa
Commando and Special Operations School (*Escuela de Comandos y Operaciones Especiales*—1986)—Coiba Island
Survival School (*Escuela de Supervivencia 'Pana-Jungla'*)—Bocas del Toro
Explosives, Demolition and Sabotage School (*Escuela de Explosivos, Demolicion y Sabotaje*—1980)—Alcalda Díaz
Frogman School (*Escuela de Hombres Rana*—1970)—Ft. Amador

Ground Forces

The Ground Force comprised four battalions plus a number of separate companies, designated Infantry,with most being structured for specialized tasks. Most had 200-plus troops usually organized into three rifle platoons (*pelotóns de fusileros*) and one or

---

[1] The COFFEE was composed of the small Units of (*Unidad de*) Commandos (*Comandos*), Frogmen (*Hombres Rana*), Explosives [Disposal] (*Explosivos*), and Special Antiterror Security Unit (see text below).
[2] Rio Hato Military Base (*Base Militar 'Gen. de Divión Omar Torrijos'*), which includes an air base, is located near the Pacific coast about 55 miles south-west of Panama City.

A lieutenant of the 2d Inf. Co. 'Diablo Rojo' during exercises. He carries US ALICE web gear and an M16A1 rifle; a full-color unit patch adorns his maroon beret. (PDF)

more supporting weapons sections and/or other specialized platoons. They were armed with a wide variety of weapons, no two being equipped the same. By 19 Dec. 1989 these units had been repositioned in expectation of some form of US intervention.

The 600- to 700-man (estimates vary and do not include the attached 1st and 2d Cos.) Bn. 2000 (*Batallón 2000*) was formed in 1984, commemorating in advance the date Panama would gain complete control of the Canal, 1 Jan. 2000. Based at Ft. Cimarrón 18 km north-east of the Torrijos/Tocumén Airports, it was intended as a mobile reaction force, some of its elements being dispersed in the hills north of Ft. Cimarrón, at Panamá La Viejo, and *La Comandancía*. It was composed of three Maneuver Cos. (*Compañias de Maniobras*): 'Eagle' ('*Aguila*'), 'Fury' ('*Furia*'), and 'Mechanized' ('*Mecanizada*'), the latter with armored

vehicles, plus the Fire Support Co. (*Compañia de Apoyo de Fuego*) with heavy mortars. Some of its training was provided by Cuban advisors.

The 1st Inf. Combat and Fire Spt. Co. 'Tiger' (*1ª Compañia de Infanteria de Combate y Apoyo de Fuego 'Tigre'* — 1959) was attached to Bn. 2000, but was not to operate as part of it. Located at Tinajitas 13 km north-north-east of Panama City, it had demonstrated exceptional loyalty to Noriega during the 3 Oct. coup attempt when it was airlifted from Rio Hato to Patilla and Tocumén Airports, by-passing US roadblocks, and then trucked to *La Comandancia*. The 2d Inf. Abn. Co. 'Puma' (*2ª Compañia de Infanteria Aerotransportada 'Puma'* — 1959), intended as a reaction force for rapid deployment within the country, was also attached to Bn. 2000. Parachute training was conducted at the Military Instruction Center. Based at the Torrijos/Tocumén

Members of the 7th Inf. Co. 'Macho de Monte' receive a Commando guidon while attending the Commando and Special Operations School (ECOE). The black-bereted ECOE cadremen wear a yellow on black 'ECOE' tab on the right shoulder. The 7th Co. soldiers wear a full-color unit patch on their camouflage berets. (PDF)

Airports[1], it was destined to defend the base, though some elements were assembled in downtown Panama City. Though considered élite, Bn. 2000's actual loyalty was questioned during the coup attempt and its performance was none too sterling during 'Just Cause'.

The 3d Inf. Co. 'Red Devils' (*3ª Compañia de Infanteria 'Diablo Rojo'* — 1969) was based in the extreme western Chiriqui Province at David near the Costa Rican border. The 4th Inf. Co. (*4ª Compañia de Infanteria 'Urraca'*, named after an Indian warrior who fought the Spanish — 1969) had supported the October coup attempt and was disbanded. The 5th and 8th Inf. Cos. (*5ª y 8ª Compañias de Infanteria*) were assigned to the MP Bn. (*Batallón de Policia Militar 'Victoriano Lorenzo'* — 1970). These companies performed normal MP duties in marked patrol cars and supplied guard dogs at critical sites, but were also

infantry trained. The 5th Co. was commanded by a West Point graduate and rabid Noriega supporter who had attempted to aid Noriega during the coup. It was located at Ft. Amador, Panama City, at the Canal's Pacific terminus, with some elements positioned west of Panama City on 20 December. The newer 8th Co. was at Ft. Espinar near the Canal's Caribbean terminus. Most of the 6th Inf. Mech. Expeditionary Co. (*6ª Compañia de Infanteria Expedicionaria Mecanizada* — 1974) and 7th Inf. Co. 'Men of the Mountain' (*7ª Compañia de Infanteria 'Macho de Monte'* — 1969) were at the Rio Hato Military Base, but elements of both reinforced *La Comandancia*, having proved their loyalty during the coup attempt. The 6th was equipped with armored vehicles; while the 7th, the most loyal of Noriega's units, was commando and special operations-trained with the main mission of forming and training guerrillas in the event of US intervention.

The 180-man Cav. Sdn. (*Escuadrón de Caballería 'Gen. José Antonio Ramon Cantera'* — 1920) was at Panamá La Viejo, on the north-east edge of Panama City; it was principally a ceremonial unit boasting a stable of 48 horses and traditional dress uniforms. The Special Antiterrorist Security Unit (*Unidad Especial de Seguridad Antiterror*, UESAT — 1980) was an élite 70-man counterterrorist force based on Flamenco Island until moved to Panamá La Viejo prior to 'Just Cause'. It also fielded a platoon-size bodyguard force directly under Noriega's aide-de-camp. Another small specialized unit was the incompletely trained

[1] The Torrijos/Tocumén Airports to the north-west of Panama City are actually two adjacent airfields, the Torrijos International Airport and the military Tocumén Air Base.

Commando Unit (*Unidad de Comandos*—1986) composed of Operational Tactical Groups A and B (*Grupos Táctico Operacional A y B*) at Ft. Espinar. There was a 50-man Military Engr. Plt. (*Pelotón de Ingenieria Militar*) and about 250 cadre, NCO students, and officer cadets at the Rio Hato Military Base.

The 400-man 2d 'Peace' Bn. (*2⁰ Batallón 'Paz'*—1985) was based in the 5th Military Zone in far north-western Chiriqui Province. Tasked with securing the Costa Rican border and local civic action, it was a low priority unit. It was composed of a Command Co. (*Compañia de Comando*) and Air Assault Cos. A 'Fortune' and B 'Minnow' (*Compañias A y B de Asalto Aéreo 'Fortuna' y 'Copal'*). The 4th Bn. (*4⁰ Batallón 'Cemaco'*, named for an Indian chief who gave Spanish colonists a rough time—1984) at Las Palmas was composed of only the 1st Mountain Co. (*1ª Compañia de Montaña*); other units could be attached in event of an emergency on the Colombian border which it was tasked to secure.

Several service support organizations also existed: the Department of Communications (*Departamento de Communicacions*—1948), War Material Service (*Servicio de Material de Guerra*—1953), Transport and Maint. Bn. (*Batallón de Transporte y Mantenimiento*—1985), and Military Medical Bn. (*Batallón de Salud Militar*—1969).

Air Force

The Panamanian Air Force traces its lineage back to a very small National Police air branch existing from 1933 to 1945. It was not until the early 1960s that the National Guard formed an air service; in 1969 this became the Panamanian Air Force (*Fuerza Aérea Panameña*—FAP), though still a component of the National Guard and later of the PDF. Flight training had been provided by Venezuela and Colombia until 1986; the FAP began its own initial training at that time, though advanced pilot and ground maintenance training was still conducted in those countries.

The FAP provided airlift, VIP transport, limited strike, recce, and coastal patrol support, while its 21 Bell 205A-1 (UH-1 Huey) helicopters principally supported the 2d Abn. Inf. Company. The 500-man FAP was equipped with a variety of commercial transports, liaison/training aircraft, and helicopters. Its fleet of short take-off and landing transports ferried supplies to outlying military zones. The FAP was organized into the Transport Sdn. (*Escuadrón de Transporte*), Rescue Sdn. (*Escuadrón de Rescate*), and Military Air Transport (*Transporte Aéro Militar*) Based principally at Tocumén and Rio Hato Air Bases. There were eight or so other airfields used by the FAP.

None of the aircraft or helicopters were airborne during 'Just Cause'. Aircraft ground crews and security personnel did contribute to the defense of the Torrijos/Tocumén and Paitilla

Demonstrating the difficulty US troops had with friend-or-foe identification, these PDF Bn. 2000 troops wear US Kevlar® helmets, US ALICE web gear, BDU-style uniforms, and carry M16A1 rifles. (PDF)

Airports. The FAP did participate in operations prior to 'Just Cause', including the use of helicopters to buzz US troops and civilians and for surveillance of US military activities. An airlift of the 1st Inf. Co. from Rio Hato to Patilla and Tocumén Airports was successfully accomplished during the coup attempt. US forces impounded 37 FAP aircraft during 'Just Cause'.

Navy

A very small navy was formed after independence, but this was permitted to dwindle away by 1923. During World War II a small Coast Guard was formed as part of the National Police, but the formation of a modern navy is considered to date from 1969. In 1984 it was redesignated the National Naval Force (*Fuerza de Marina Nacional*—FMN) with headquarters at Ft. Amador, the Pacific elements based at Balboa, and the Caribbean elements at Colón. At the time of 'Just Cause' the 500-man FMN operated eight coastal patrol craft, five landing craft, two logistics support ships (converted landing craft), and a 150-man capacity troop transport (converted shrimp boat). The 1st Naval Inf. Co. (*1ª Compañia de Infanteria de Marina*) was based at Coco Solo on the Caribbean side and the new Naval Commando Plt. (*Pelotón Comandos de Marina*) was at Ft. Amador.

A 2d Bn. 'Paz' Soviet 14.5 mm ZPU-4 quad anti-aircraft machine gun in Chiriqui Province. These were used to engage the

Rangers' C-130s as they dropped on Rio Hato. (PDF)

Police and paramilitary units

The Panamanian Police Force (*Fuerza de Policia*, FP—1913) was formed from the law enforcement elements of the old National Guard. They performed typical local law enforcement and highway patrol duties throughout the country. After 1983 the FP, consisting of about 5,000 personnel, were subordinate to the PDF. The FP maintained stations in the cities while the rural areas were under the jurisdiction of police subordinate to the military zones. Police training was conducted at PDF facilities and they maintained a Police Academy. FP armament consisted principally of handguns and assault rifles. Two well-armed rapid deployment civil disturbance companies, often referred to as public order units, were formed in 1986 and 1988; 1st and 2d Anti-riot Cos. (*1ª y 2ª Compañias de Antimotines 'Doberman' y 'Centurion'*). The 1st was disbanded after the October coup attempt due to its failure to support Noriega. The 2d assisted the defense of *La Comandancia* on 20 December 1989. Other components of the FP included the National Director of Ground Traffic (*Dirección Nacional de Tránsito Terrestre*, DNTT—1983) and Highway Patrol (*Patrulla de Caminos*—1964), both of which maintained stations throughout the country.

The 1,500-man National Department of Investigation (*Departamento de Nacional de Investigaciones*, DENI—1960) was actually a secret police organization maintaining a network of informers among the population and within Panamanian government agencies, and undercover agents among civilian employees of the Panama Canal Commission and US armed forces. The final FP organization, the National Guard (*Guardia Nacional*),

was composed of the Presidential Guard (*Guardia Presidencial*— 1941), Penitentiary Guard (*Guardia Penitenciaria*—1925), Port Guard Force (*Fuerza de Policia Portuaria*—1984), and Forest Guard (*Guardia Forestal*—1979).

This profileration of non-military organizations under the PDF existed principally to broaden Noriega's power base and span of control over the Panamanian people. It was more a Mafia-style organization than a true military force, with no system of checks and balances. It also diluted the effectiveness of the PDF and proved to harbor numerous personnel of questionable loyalty to Noriega.

The mis-named **'Dignity Battalions'** (*Batallóns de la Dignidad*) were a paramilitary group organized in March 1988 by Noriega in a fairly successful ploy to gain popular support from the lower class unemployed and peasants. Civil servants were also bullied by their supervisors into participating in training as a show of support for the regime. Convicted criminals also served, being released from jail in exchange for signing up. Though most were unpaid volunteers, some did receive a small salary. The battalions were an effort to create a psychological impact on the Panamanian population and US, supposedly demonstrating the people's support of Noriega and serving notice that US troops would be faced by a united hostile population. These non-uniformed units were administered by the PDF through a simple 'Dignity Brigade Staff' headed by picked government employees.

US intelligence abbreviated the battalions as 'Dig Bats'; they were quickly dubbed 'Dingbats' by US troops. About 11 'battalions' were formed, with anything from 24 to 250 volunteers each and bearing such patriotic names as 'Christopher Columbus', 'Latin Liberation', and 'St. Michael the Archangel'. About half were in the Panama City area with most of the others around Rio Hato, Colón, and Ft. Cimarrón. Another seven 'battalions' existed on paper, principally in outlying areas. Total strength of the Dig Bats was never accurately determined, with official estimates ranging from 2,000 to 3,000 armed civilians, though many of these failed to participate actively in defense of Noriega's regime.

None were well enough motivated nor trained to pose a real threat. Training was extremely rudimentary and included weapon familiarization, simple hand-to-hand combat, and drill. This was conducted principally by active and retired PDF officers and NCOs, some of whom fought with their 'units'. Modeled after the Nicaraguan Popular Militia and the old Cuban National Revolutionary Militia, some cadre training was provided by Nicaraguan and Cuban special forces personnel (headed by José Antonio Arbesu Fraga, now assigned as Chief of the Cuban Interests Section, Embassy of Czechoslovakia in Washington).

Though armed with assault rifles, other automatic weapons and RPG rocket launchers, the Dig Bats' low level of training and lack of military discipline rendered them more of a nuisance than a threat to US forces. None operated as a cohesive unit and the few who actually fought operated in small roving bands. Apart

Wearing civilian clothing as part of their rôle as guerrillas, 2d Bn. 'Paz' troops patrol in an ex-US *M151 jeep mounting a Czechoslovak 7.92 mm ZB-53 machine gun. (PDF)*

Taiwanese T-65 rifles carried by troops of the 6th Military Zone (Coclé Province) Reaction

Platoon 'Indio'; they wear their subdued unit patch on camouflage berets. (PDF)

from random sniping and a few scattered harassing attacks, the main problems caused by the Dig Bats were looting, arson, attacks on political opposition, and the simple settling of old scores with fellow Panamanians. US news media often over-inflated their strength and portrayed them as more important than they actually were, since commanders were sometimes forced to disperse their troops over wide areas to prevent looting and to protect the population and their own lines of communications.

Intelligence

The PDF's intelligence efforts were largely directed inward in search of disloyalty in its own ranks. Relying principally on informers, the counter-intelligence net was of only limited effectiveness. It was even less effective in collecting intelligence on US forces, though the PDF was relatively successful in tracking US movements (until the final days before 'Just Cause', when full US counter-intelligence and deception efforts were launched). Huge amounts of data were collected by a disorderly system without central direction and control. Noriega, not trusting others and relying on his admittedly extensive G-2 background, insisted on processing and analyzing this mass of confused data himself. Unable to do so, he believed until the end that the US would not actually launch a major military operation against him.

However, Noriega did have a small intelligence operation that remained undetected by the US until after 'Just Cause'. It was headed by Capt. Asunción Eliezer Gaitan, considered one of the most cunning and ruthless of Noriega's henchmen, who served as a go-between with the Cubans, Nicaraguans, and Colombian drug cartels. The US and Panama have not seen the last of him.

Deployment

In the weeks prior to 'Just Cause' Noriega dispersed some units and constantly relocated elements in an effort to confuse US intelligence and increase their chances of survival in event of US action. This had a poor effect on PDF troops, causing a drop in morale which was aggravated by the effect of US pro-active exercises prior to D-Day. The PDF lacked both a cohesive plan to employ these widely dispersed units effectively, and capable senior officers, trusted by the troops, to conduct a viable defence. They were also hampered by lack of reliable long-range communications.

Due to Noriega's lack of trust in much of the PDF, and in order not to have to rely on a single unit's loyalty, he had assembled an *ad hoc* force to defend *La Comandancía*. Equivalent to two-plus companies, this force comprised personnel of the 2d Anti-riot Co., 6th and 7th Inf. Cos., Bn. 2000, and UESAT, plus a few loyal personnel from the disbanded 1st Anti-riot and 4th Inf. Companies.

Equipment

Though the PDF lacked any modern heavy crew-served weapon systems, they did boast a number of US-made Cadillac Gage Commando wheeled armored vehicles purchased in 1983–84: four V-150 command vehicles, 13 V-150 armored personnel carriers (APC), and 13 V-300 APC, fire support, and recovery variants. These vehicles were allotted to the 6th Inf. Mech. Co. (2 × V-150s, 9 × V-150 APCs, 4 × V-300s) and to Bn. 2000's Mech. Co. (2 × V-150s, 4 × V-150 APCs, 9 × V-300s), though on 20 Dec. 1989 many were dispersed to varied locations and had frequently been moved about.

The PDF possessed a wide range of small arms and light crew-served weapons, principally of US, Soviet, Warsaw Pact, Western European, and Israeli origins, the Eastern Bloc equipment being provided by Cuba and Nicaragua. The predominant individual weapons were Soviet and other Warsaw Pact-made 7.62 mm AK-47 and AKM assault rifles. The previously standard 5.56 mm US M16A1 and the similar Taiwanese T-65 rifles were somewhat older, and were being replaced by AKs; but some units were still armed with these, and others were issued to the Dig Bats along with AKs. Other common weapons were Belgian 7.62 mm FN FAL rifles, Israeli 9 mm Uzi sub-machine guns. various shotguns, and 9 mm pistols—the latter in far greater abundance than typically issued to armed forces. Both US M21 and Soviet SVD sniper rifles were used. Grenade-launchers included the US M79 and M203 plus the West German H & K grenade pistol, all 40 mm. Some obsolete US shoulder weapons from the National Guard days were encountered, such as Garand M1 rifles, M1 and M2 carbines, and Thompson M1928A1 sub-machine guns. Both US and Soviet hand grenades were used.

Rifle-caliber machine guns included US .30-cal. M1919A4s, US 7.62 mm M60s, Czechoslovak 7.92 mm ZB-53s, and Belgian 7.62 mm MAGs, along with some heavy US .50-cal. M2s. Some 20 Soviet 14.5 mm ZPU-4 quad anti-aircraft machine guns were also available; there were no heavier air defense guns or missile

systems, and the only 'air warning' radar available to the PDF were standard air traffic control radars. Limited anti-armour protection was provided by large quantities of Soviet RPG-2, -7, and -18 rocket launchers (the latter a one-shot disposable model similar to the US LAW), which were also used against helicopters. Other anti-armour weapons included a few US 90 mm M67 and Chinese 75 mm Type 52 (copy of US M20) recoilless rifles, French 89 mm LARC-89, and even some obsolete US 3.5-inch M20A1B1 rocket launchers ('bazooka'). There were no modern wire-guided anti-tank missile systems. The PDF possessed no artillery, but relied on mortars including 60 mm US M2s and Israeli Soltams, plus a handful of US 81 mm M29s and 4.2-inch M30s, and French 120 mm RT-61s. Over 76,500 weapons were eventually captured, confiscated, or turned in—over five times the numbers needed to arm the entire PDF, and Noriega's future plans can only be guessed at.

* * *

Under Noriega the PDF had turned into a corrupt military machine resorting to brutality, terror, and theft against its own citizens. Unpopular with the people they exploited, they were derogatorily referred to as '*La Botas*' (The Boots). The PDF and its subordinate 'non-military' organizations (exclusive of the Dig Bats) numbered approximately 15,000 uniformed personnel (including women in the military and FP), but only about 6,000 were combat troops. Noriega was in the process of expanding the PDF even further, having announced in 1985 that it would eventually grow to 25,000, and there were plans to purchase 60

Support troops of one of the ten 10th Military Zone (La Chorrera Province) detachments, wearing olive green fatigues and US M1 helmets with both camouflage covers and nets. They wear subdued military zone shoulder tabs (10ª ZONA); full-color tabs are yellow on red. (PDF)

Argentine TAM tanks. The programme included the expansion of existing units, the formation of a Bn. 'Atlantic', plus Railway, Customs, and Coastal Island Guards. The PDF's 1989 budget of $150,000,000 was reduced to $80,000,000 by the new government.

JOINT TASK FORCE SOUTH

The composition of units that were to make up JTFSO demonstrated the US Army's organizational flexibility and interoperability so critical for the success of fluid contingency operations. Though some units had the opportunity to plan and rehearse the operation's initial phase jointly, most had no such chance. The first contingency plans for the commitment of troops in event of an emergency were developed in Feb. 1988, Operation Plan 'Blue Spoon'. This plan allowed for the defense of US installations, civil military operations, evacuation of non-

Male and female Dignity Battalion members, armed with T-65 rifles, parade in their red T-shirts, dark slacks, and tennis shoes. (PDF)

combatant personnel, and the neutralization of the PDF. In the event JTFSO, besides conducting civil military operations (i.e. providing military support of civil authorities and public services), also began training the Panama Public Forces, the replacement for the Police Force, within days of the operation's beginning.

From March 1988 the first of four deployments of US troops to Panama, for security enhancement and to insure the 1978 Panama Canal Treaties were maintained, took place with the introduction of additional MP and aviation units. In April additional units were deployed and Joint Task Force Panama was activated on 9 April. In May the XVIII Abn. Corps was designated as the base formation for Joint Task Force South (JTFSO) and made responsible for planning and executing joint contingency operations in Panama. After the illegal May 1989 elections 1,900 more troops were deployed during Operation 'Nimrod Dancer', joining 10,300 already there. Units from the 7th Inf. and 82d Abn. Divs. were rotated at three- to six-month intervals as part of 'Nimrod Sustain'. Many of the units went through the Jungle Operations Training Center and did much to develop the initial ground work for 'Just Cause' preparations. Through the summer of 1989 planning for possible military operations was intensified. Joint training and freedom of movement exercises began to be conducted, Exercises 'Sand Flea' and 'Purple Storm'. In Nov. 1989 OPLAN 'Blue Spoon' was revised due to the PDF ability to respond demonstrated during the October coup attempt, and was now called OPLAN 90-2; this would become Operation 'Just Cause'.

Units were contributed by a wide range of formations including several different brigades, divisions, corps, and other major commands. The units of today's Army are assigned or attached to the many large formations and commands for administration and, to the extent possible, to those with which wartime contingency plans expect them to deploy. These assignments and attachments are by no means permanent or inviolate; the Army is structured and trained to permit units to be cross-attached to other commands in whatever combination the mission may require. Peacetime chains-of-command that smaller units normally fall under are by-passed, and they come under the operational control of the command to which they are attached, even though they are still assigned administratively to their parent headquarters. Units are selected for attachment to contingency formations depending on the operation's need for particular types of units, their geographic location, equipment readiness, and current levels of training. This 'building block' principle of assembling units into mission-oriented task forces is one of the key reasons for 'Just Cause's' success.

The overall 'on the ground' headquarters responsible for 'Just Cause' was US Southern Command (USSOUTHCOM), headquartered at Quarry Heights within Panama City and commanded by Gen. Maxwell R. Thurman, who had only assumed command at the end of September. USSOUTHCOM is a unified joint service command responsible for overseeing US military operations throughout Latin America[1]. The XVIII Abn. Corps at Ft. Bragg, NC, commanded by Lt. Gen. Carl W. Stiner, provided the ground maneuver force headquarters for JTFSO. As such, a number of JTFSO's units were subordinate to the corps, though many other corps units were not committed to the operation[2]. Other units, however, were drawn from other major commands

---

[1] USSOUTHCOM's area of responsibility includes Central and South America and the Caribbean basin. Though responsible for planning contingency missions in its AO, most of its efforts are directed to the defense of the Canal, and providing training, advisory and civil assistance missions to many Latin American countries.
[2] XVIII Abn. Corps is composed of 10th Mountain Div. (Lt. Inf.)—Ft. Drum, NY; 24th Inf. Div. (Mech)—Ft. Stewart, Ga.; 82d Abn. Div.; 101st Abn. Div. (Air Assault)—Ft. Campbell, Ky.; 194th Armd. Bde. (Sep)—Ft. Knox, Ky.; 197th Inf. Bde. (Mech) (Sep)—Ft. Benning, Ga.; 16th MP Bde. (Abn); 18th FA Bde. (Abn); 18th Avn. Bde. (Abn); 20th Engr. Bde. (Abn); 35th Sig. Bde. (Abn); 525th MI Bde (Abn). (Units without a location are at Ft. Bragg, NC.)

including: US Army Forces Command (FORSCOM), Third US Army, I and III Corps, US Army South (USARSO), and US Army Special Operations Command (USASOCOM). Units were also drawn from divisions and brigades themselves not committed to 'Just Cause'.

The major ground maneuver formations (brigade equivalent and larger) committed to 'Just Cause' were the 7th Inf. Div. (Lt)—Ft. Ord, Calif.; 1st Bde., 82d Abn. Div.—Ft. Bragg; 193d Inf. Bde. (Lt) (Sep)—Panama; and 75th Ranger Regt.—Ft. Benning, Ga. (with battalions located elsewhere). However, as will be seen, not all of these formations' subordinate units were under their control during 'Just Cause'. In all, 26,000 US personnel were committed, including 13,000 (9,500 Army) assigned to USSOUTHCOM in-place in Panama on 20 Dec., and another 13,000 (10,500 Army) committed from the States. Of these, 1,700 Rangers and 3,300 paratroopers jumped in the largest airborne operation since World War II. Interestingly, some 770 female soldiers served in combat support and combat service support units, with a number becoming actively engaged in combat.

The principal tactical maneuver formations employed during 'Just Cause' were task organized into multi-battalion task forces. The main task forces (TFs Atlantic, Bayonet, Pacific, Red) were uniquely organized, with different mixes of combat and combat support elements structured to accomplish their assigned missions. (Designations of TFs are somewhat confusing since some were composed of smaller TFs.)

Light infantry battalions provided the bulk of the committed maneuver units. There are four types of light infantry battalions: Airborne (42 officers, 636 enlisted), Light (36 officers, 524 enlisted), and Ranger (44 officers, 531 enlisted); Air Assault Battalions did not participate. Though similar in organization, each has a slightly different internal structure, weapons mix, and intended mission. Airborne and Light Infantry Battalions possess a Headquarters and Headquarters Company (HHC) composed of a Battalion Headquarters (HQ); Staff Sections; Scout, Mortar (four 81 mm M252 or M29A1), Communications, Support (supply, transport, mess), and Medical Platoons; only airborne battalions have a Maintenance Section. The light battalion HHCs also have an Antiarmor Platoon (TOW); airborne battalions have instead a TOW missile-equipped Antiarmor Company (Co. D). The three Ranger Battalions' HHCs are rather austere possessing only a Battalion HQ; Staff Sections; Fire Support (forward observers), Communications, Support, and Medical Platoons.

Each type of battalion has three Rifle Companies (A, B, C) with an HQ and three Rifle Platoons comprising an HQ and three Rifle Squads. The nine-man Rifle Squads (the same in all battalions) are armed with seven 5.56 mm M16A2 rifles, two of which mount 40 mm M203 grenade launchers, and two 5.56 mm M249E1 squad automatic weapons (SAW). Additionally, they carry a mix of hand grenades and Light Antitank Weapons (LAW): the 66 mm M72A3 and/or the deadly new 84 mm M136.

Distribution of crew-served weapons within the different types of companies differs. In Airborne Rifle Companies the two 60 mm M224 lightweight mortars are in the Mortar Section. There are two 7.62 mm M60 machine guns and two M47 Dragon missile teams in the Rifle Platoons' Weapons Squad. Light Rifle Companies have both Mortar and Antiarmor Sections as part of the Company HQ, the latter with six Dragon teams for attachment to the Rifle Platoons/Squads. Two M60 teams are in each Platoon HQ for attachment to squads. Ranger Rifle Companies have a Weapons Platoon with Mortar and Antiarmor Sections. The latter was equipped with three Dragons and/or six 90 mm M67 recoilless rifles, the mix determined by mission requirements. The Rifle Platoons have a Machine Gun Squad

A 4-6th Inf. track driver rests in his M113A3 APC. He is wearing an older model M69 body armor vest. (DoD)

with three M60 teams. All units (except the Rangers) deployed with their HMMWV-mounted[1] M220A1 TOW (Tube-launched Optically tracked Wire command-link) and man-packed Dragon wire-guided antiarmor missile sytems in case PDF armored vehicles were encountered. Once in-country most of these systems were left with support elements and the TOW crews used as mounted scouts or security (the TOWs usually replaced by .50-cal. M2 machine guns), and the Dragon gunners reinforced the Rifle Platoons. Full compliments of mortars were also taken, but again these were seldom used due to the need to limit collateral damage, and the crews were used as security elements.

A single Mechanized Infantry Battalion (47 officers, 766 enlisted) was deployed from the 5th Inf. Div. (Mech) at Ft. Polk, La. The augmented 4th Bn. (Mech), 6th Inf. Regt. (TF 4-6) was equipped with the older M113A3 armored personnel carrier (APC) rather than the modern M2 Bradley infantry fighting vehicle[2]. Its HHC is composed of the same elements as the Airborne Infantry Battalion's plus an almost company-size Maintenance Platoon, and is transported by 43 full-tracked vehicles and 109 various trucks—considerably more vehicles than in an entire airborne battalion. The Heavy Mortar Platoon has six M106A2 self-propelled mortar carriers mounting 107 mm

(4.2-inch) M30 mortars. There are four Rifle Companies each with a Company HQ, three Rifle Platoons, and an Antiarmor Section with two M901 Improved TOW Vehicles (ITV—twin TOWs on a modified M113). The Rifle Platoons are transported in four M113A3 APCs, one each for the HQ and three Rifle Squads; each APC mounts a .50-cal. M2 machine gun. The Rifle Squads are armed the same as their light counterparts, but with the addition of an organic Dragon. There are no company-level mortars. The ITV-equipped Co. E (Antiarmor) was not deployed to Panama. Some of TF 4-6's APCs were detached to other units for armored transport and fire support.

Besides the mechanized battalion's APCs, the Army's only armored vehicles deployed to Panama were from the 82d Abn. Div.'s Co. C, 3d Bn. (Lt) (Abn), 73d Armor Regiment. The M551A1 Sheridan light airborne assault vehicles, air-droppable light tanks, date from the early 1960s. Their main gun/launcher is capable of firing either a conventional 152 mm projectile or a Shillelagh wire-guided missile. They also mount .50-cal. M2 and 7.62 mm M240C machine guns. Those of 3-73 Armor are the only combat operational Sheridans still in use by the Army. While of immense value during 'Just Cause', they are not exactly current state-of-the-art systems. Having proved their value due to their air deployable capability, and their ability to maneuver easily in close built-up areas and deliver decisive firepower quickly, the Army has been enticed to speed up its long postponed Armored Gun System programme to field a modern replacement.

Army Special Operations Forces (SOF) played a widely varied and valuable rôle in 'Just Cause'. The organization most closely associated with SOF is Special Forces. The resident SF unit in Panama was 3d Bn., 7th Special Forces Group (Abn) (SFGA)

[1] HMMWV ('Hum-Vee')—High Mobility Multipurpose Wheeled Vehicle, a robust 5/4-ton four-wheel-drive utility truck, which replaced the 1/4-ton utility truck, or 'jeep'.

[2] See Osprey Vanguards 34, *M113 Series*, and 43, *M2 Bradley*

ationed at Ft. Davis. The remainder of the 7th SFGA is based
t Ft. Bragg, though its Co. A, 1st Bn. reinforced the 3d. The
emainder of the Group was committed on 30 Dec. 1989. An SF
Battalion is composed of a Battalion HQ, more commonly known
s an SF Operational Detachment-C or, simply, C-Team,
omprising only various staff sections. Each of the three SF
Companies has an HQ, or B-Team, and six 12-man A-Teams.
The SF Battalion Support Company is composed of an HQ plus
Military Intelligence, Service, and Signal Detachments, while a
imilar but larger Support Company services the SFGA.

Other SOF units committed to 'Just Cause' included the 4th
Psyops. Grp.'s 1st Psyops. Bn. (+) (Joint Psyops. TF); 96th
Civil Affairs Bn. (−) (Joint CA TF); 617th Avn. Det. (Special
Ops); elements of 160th Avn. Grp. (Special Ops) (TF 160) with
2 AH-6 Little Bird, 10 MH-6, 7 MH-47E, 17 MH-60K Night
Hawk special ops. helicopters; and 1st SF Operational Det.-D,
nore commonly known as 'Delta Force'. Principally a counter-
errorist unit, the highly classified 'Delta Force' is also tasked
with contingency direct action and recovery missions. The 7th
SFGA, 75th Ranger Regt., TF 160, 'Delta Force', and Navy
SEALS were under the control of Special Operations Command,
South (SOCSOUTH), together forming the Joint Special Operations
TF (JSOTF).

The **US Marine Corps** provided a small but invaluable
attalion-sized special purpose force. The 724-man (including 18
USN) Marine Forces, Panama (MarFor, Panama), was composed of three specialized companies, later augmented by a
fourth. Additionally, a small Marine Security Guard Det.
protected the US Embassy. The Marines are armed with
essentially the same weapons as the Army, but field a few unique
models. Co. D (+), 2d Lt. Armd. Inf. Bn. proved itself of
particular value with its 17 LAV-series light armored vehicles—
eight-wheeled armored cars. The 14 LAV-25s mount a 25 mm
chain gun, two 7.62 mm machine guns, and transport a scout
team. Like the Sheridans they provided protected mobility, high-
speed response in congested areas, and direct fire support. (The
Army, which had earlier dropped out of the joint LAV project,
was impressed enough with the vehicle that it has since leased
some from the Marines for issue to the 82d Abn. Division.)

Heavy use was made of **Army aviation** attack, utility, cargo,
and observation helicopters (UH-1H Iroquois or, more
popularly, Huey), AH-1S Cobra, CH-47C Chinook, OH-56A/C
Kiowa, UH-60A Black Hawk, AH-64 Apache). The Avn. Bde.,
7th Inf. Div. and XVIII Abn. Corps' 18th Avn. Bde. HQs
controlled a mix of aviation units subordinate to TF Aviation.

*Camouflaged members of
the 1/75th Rangers check
their parachutes during in-
flight rigging aboard a*
*C-141 en route from
Hunter Army Airfield to
Tocumén/Torrijos
Airports, Panama. (DoD)*

A 5-87th Inf. M203 grenade launcher-armed grenadier in Balboa. He wears a grenade carrier vest over his PASGT body armor vest. (SSG P. Prater)

Rifle squad members rest on an M956 TOW missile carrier HMMWV of 5-87th Inf.s' Antiarmor Platoon. From the left they are armed with an M249E1 SAW, M16A2 rifle, and M203 grenade launcher. (SSG P. Prater)

The full spectrum of Army **combat support units** were committed. These units, which generally received little publicity, were invaluable combat multipliers, bringing their special abilities and equipment to the battlefield and included: light field artillery (105 mm M102 howitzers), air defense artillery (20 mm M167 Vulcan guns used in a ground fire rôle), combat engineers, signal, military police, and military intelligence. Joint Intelligence TF was under the control of the Panama-based 470th MI Bde. and supplemented by XVIII Abn. Corps' 525th MI Bde. (Abn)(−).

Combat service support units were also extremely important. Though many were undermanned, they were able to provide the critical logistical support to the combat and combat support elements. The ordnance and aviation maintenance, transportation (truck and landing craft), quartermaster supply, medical, administrative, and forward support units were either deployed from the US with their parent units or were already in-place in Panama. Most were subordinate to XVIII Abn. Corps' 1st Corps Support Command (1st COSCOM) under which were the 41st Area Spt. Gp. and 44th Medical Bde. (−). Over 300 individual Army Reservists were committed to 'Just Cause', principally in support of civil-military operations.

'Just Cause' was the first US military operation in which the forces found themselves armed with a large number of **foreign-designed weapons**, most of which are manufactured in the US under license. Until the mid-1970s the US military relied solely on native weapon designs. It was not until rising development and procurement costs, NATO standardization efforts, negotiated procurement trade-offs between different countries, rapidly improving technology in many countries, and the development of some very good ideas across the ocean, that the US began to look overseas for some of its weaponry. Included are 7.62 mm M240C/M240E1 machine guns on the Sheridan and LAV-25 (Belgian FN tank MAG), 5.56 mm M249E1 SAW (Belgian FN Minimi), 9 mm M9 pistol (Italian Beretta 92F), 84 mm M136 LAW (Swedish AT-4), improved 81 mm M252 mortar (British L16A1), 83 mm MK 153 MOD 0 Shoulder-launched Multi-purpose Assault Weapon (SMAW) (based on Israeli B-300 rocket launcher), and LAV-series light armored vehicles (Swiss-designed, Canadian-built); the latter two systems were used only by the Marines.

Applied experience

Training was the key to JTFSO's success. Army training programs, unit and joint exercises, and rotations through Combat Training Centers provide challenges, demand flexibility, and tax units under simulated but realistic combat conditions. The Combat Training Centers, such as the National Training Center at Ft. Irwin, Calif. (principally for high-intensity heavy forces, though light units also participate) and the Joint Readiness Training Center at Ft. Chaffee, Ark. (for low- and mid-intensity light and special operations forces), provide especially rigorous and challenging exercises, pitting the units against an unco-operative and highly proficient Opposing Force.

Lessons learned from the many exercises, combat training centers, and actual recent conflicts are intensely studied. Overseas deployment exercises are extremely critical. The

logistics and co-ordination demands of long-range deployment is one of the most difficult tasks facing a unit. This training was to serve units well when it came to the short-notice deployment to Panama. Unit training concentrates on many factors that also contributed to 'Just Cause's' success, including military operations in urban terrain (all troop posts have mock towns for this purpose), organic weapons and fire support employment, and small unit actions placing a high degree of emphasis on junior leaders' initiative. Units conducted critical training prior to deployment in the form of aggressive live fire exercises and battle drills, many of them at night. Strict rules of engagement were developed to prevent civilian casualties and limit collateral damage. Situational training exercises were developed to insure soldiers had a complete understanding of the rules.

At higher command levels, much was learned from the co-ordination problems encountered between the different services during the 1983 Grenada operation, 'Urgent Fury'[1]. Though some problems still exist, many had been eliminated and the overall operation developed rather smoothly[2].

US Air Force participation in 'Just Cause' was substantial, and crucial to the operation's success. The Tactical Air Command provided fighter and attack aircraft close air support as well as Tactical Air Control Parties (TACP) to direct their strikes from the ground. Military Airlift Command (MAC) transports, from 21 different airlift wings from around the country, conducted a massive lift of troops, equipment, and supplies as well as executing numerous parachute drops. A total of 111 airlift sorties[3] were flown to airdrop and airland the strike forces and

A 5-87th Inf. company command post operating from an M998 cargo/troop carrier HMMWV in Balboa. (DoD)

1st Bde., 7th Inf. Div. 'Light Fighters' arriving at Howard AFB and preparing to board CH-47C Chinook helicopters for deployment into Panama City, 23 December 1989. (DoD)

[1] See Osprey MAA 159, *Grenada 1983*.
[2] For additional information on the Army's organization and weapons, see Elite 20, *Inside the US Army Today*.
[3] A sortie is a single flight by one aircraft.

,000 tons of supplies and equipment on 20 Dec. alone. MAC also provided Combat Control Teams (CCT), the Air Force's pathfinders; and MAC aeromedical evacuation units flew casualties back to the States. Between 20 Dec. 1989 and 1 Jan. 1990 the USAF flew 399 sorties, lifting in 19,500 personnel and 21,900 tons of cargo. By the end of 'Just Cause' on 31 Jan. 1990 775 missions had been flown. Three C-141s and 11 C-130s had been slightly damaged by ground fire. The Strategic Air Command (SAC) provided tanker aircraft from 26 refueling squadrons. Several security police squadrons assisted with in-country air base security.

The 1st Special Operations Wing (1st SOW) from Hurlbert Field, Fla., flew scores of specialized mission sorties with nine AC-130 Spectre gunships[1], five other specialized C-130 variants, five MH-53J Pave Low III helicopters, and four MH-60G Pave Hawk helicopters. Some of these aircraft were in-place on D Day and others deployed after its start.

The headquarters for USAF units permanently based at Howard and Albrook Air Force Bases is USAF South and its 2,400-man 830th Air Div., controlling the 24th Combat Spt. Grp., 24th Medical Grp., and 24th Composite Wing. The latter's 24th Tactical Spt. Sdn. is equipped with 21 OA-37B Dragonfly observation/ground attack jets, which flew 255 sorties during 'Just Cause'. The 830th Air Div.'s 61st Military Airlift Wing is equipped with C-22, C-130, and contracted Spanish-built CASA 212 transports. The organization also operates the Inter-

The seven committed AC-130Hs mounted two 20 mm Vulcans, a 40 mm cannon, and a 105 mm howitzer. The two AC-130As of the USAF Reserve's 919th Spl. Ops. Grp., Duke Field, Fla., were similarly armed except that the 105 mm was replaced by another 40 mm plus two 7.62 mm Miniguns.

American Air Forces Academy involved with training Latin American air forces.

Two tactical fighter units were temporarily in Panama prior to the operation. Several unarmed F-16A Fighting Falcons of the 388th Tactical Fighter Wing from Hill AFB, Utah, were flying intercept missions against suspected drug flights from South America. These aircraft were flown back to the States on 21 Dec. since they were unable to contribute to the operation, and to prevent them from being attacked on the ground. Elements of the Air National Guard's 180th Tactical Fighter Grp. from Toledo, Ohio, were conducting their two-week annual training in Panama when 'Just Cause' began. The unit's A-7D Corsair II ground attack aircraft flew 76 invaluable close air support sorties, delivering 20 mm cannon fire. A great deal of publicity was given the use of six (originally reported as two) F-117A Stealth fighters from the 37th Tactical Fighter Wing, Tonopah Test Range, Nev., two of which preceded the Ranger-carrying C-130 transports into Rio Hato. Other than two 2000-lb bombs dropped by F-117As at Rio Hato and 2.75-inch smoke marking rockets launched from OA-37Bs, no USAF air-to-ground ordnance was delivered other than machine gun and cannon fire. Three E-3A Sentry Airborne Warning and Control System (AWACS) aircraft, along with a number of F-15 Eagles, were committed to interdict Noriega if he attempted to escape by air.

US Navy participation, under Naval Forces, Panama, was limited, with only 600 personnel present. Among these were SEAL (Sea-Air-Land commando) Teams from Naval Special Warfare Units 2 and 8 plus Special Boat Unit 26, subordinate to the US Navy Special Warfare Command. Elements of the SEAL Teams made up TFs White, Blue, and Green, which arrived in

Panama just prior to the operation. SEAL Teams are composed of 11 SEAL Platoons (designated by phonetic letters) with three eight-man squads.

'MAXIMUM LEADER'

Manuel Antonio Noriega's relationship with the US was unfortunately a long one. Born illegitimately in 1938 in the slums of Panama City, he was raised in Chiriqui Province where he learned some of the Indians' ways, along with voodoo, which he practised. He managed to secure a commission in the National Guard in the late 1950s; and reportedly, was recruited by the CIA while attending the Peruvian Military Academy in the early 1960s. It was not long before he was thought to be on the payroll of several countries' intelligence services.

Dec. 1969 found Noriega as the commander of the backwater Province of Chiriqui on the Costa Rican border. A timely demonstration of support for Gen. Torrijos at a time of crisis bought him the reward of the post of G-2 (Intelligence), one of the most powerful positions in the National Guard. He held this post until appointed commander-in-chief in 1983, all the time continuing his double-dealing with the various intelligence communities. In 1976 Torrijos directed Lt. Col. Noriega to prepare plans to sabotage the Canal and attack US military

headquarters in the event that negotiations over the Canal's future failed. Following a public announcement by the Director of the CIA that he was removed from its payroll, Noriega, cut off from the payments he so valued, directed his best efforts toward the Cubans, fell in with the drug cartels, and became involved with drug trafficking and drug money laundering. He was active during the political turmoil in the aftermath of Torrijos' death (in which he may have had a hand). Appointed commander-in-chief in 1983, he promoted himself to brigadier general and set about reorganizing and corrupting the National Guard, renaming it the Defense Forces of Panama. By 1985 he was established as the *de facto* ruler of Panama. He permitted the exploitation of the population through kickbacks to selected PDF officers and government officials from virtually all government services, ranging from drivers' licenses fees to public transportation fares. Noriega reinforced the loyalty of the PDF by promoting Indian and Spanish-Indian officers and enlisted men, often passed over in the past, and making available to the forces scarce consumer goods. His intimidation of the political class and scarcely concealed corruption of most state institutions led in 1986 to riots which served as his pretext for declaring martial law. Public protests became a common event, usually brutally suppressed by Noriega's forces. Opposition newspapers were closed and some of Noriega's enemies exiled. By now Noriega was considered the

'Task Force Red Devil' paratroopers of 1-508th Inf. assemble PDF prisoners outside Ft. *Amador near the Bridge of the Americas spanning the Canal. (DoD)*

wealthiest man in Panama, with ill-gotten assets estimated between $200 and $600 million. In Sept. 1987 the US Senate passed a resolution urging Panama to re-establish a civilian government, followed by a second resolution cutting military and economic aid. Panama countered by alleging the US violation of the Canal treaties, and began to restrict US military presence.

From 1987, aided by Cuban and Nicaraguan psyops experts, Noriega conducted a well-orchestrated campaign against his opponents. Using intimidation, disinformation, falsified documents and rumors, the PDF attempted to vilify and ridicule US troops and commercial interests as well as the Panamanian opposition. Newspapers, films, posters, television, and radio were the media used to transmit the hate messages, some of them intelligently devised. Though the campaign failed to gain the support of most Panamanians or seriously to affect US morale, it was unrelenting and had begun to wear on its audiences.

The Colombian Medellin drug cartel operated freely in Panama under Noriega's protection. Organized armed bands operating in Panama City and Darien Province on the Colombian border were involved in the transport of drugs and the operation of drug labs, and were instrumental to Noriega's accumulation of wealth. He also supported, principally by arms smuggling on behalf of Cuba and Nicaragua, Salvadorean Communist guerrillas and Colombia's M-19 (*Movimiento 19 de Abril*) terrorists. In Feb. 1988 US federal grand juries indicted Noriega on drug trafficking charges, protection of cocaine shipments to the US, and racketeering. There were even two indictments accusing Noriega of accepting bribes of $4.6 and $5.4 million. With no extradition agreements existing between the US and Panama,

there was little hope of Noriega being turned over to authorities. The US placed pressure on the weak President Delvalle to fire Noriega; he did so on national television, but Noriega was in a stronger position than many realized. The next day he simply dismissed Delvalle and his vice-president, placing the loyal Manuel Palma in the president's chair.

Strikes and protests continued, and Noriega closed all opposition news media. The US still recognized Delvalle as president and reacted quickly, with courts freezing Panamanian funds in US banks; the government imposed economic sanctions and withheld Canal fee payments to the illegal regime. To further ensure the loyalty of the PDF, Noriega protected its pay from these sanctions. Though his speeches were filled with accusations of 'American imperialism', only two regional states recognized his government—Cuba and Nicaragua. The situation was serious enough that the US began planning for contingency operations. In April 1988, after a failed coup by Panamanian Police officers, President Reagan instituted further economic sanctions against Panama and troop reinforcements were deployed to secure US facilities.

On 12 April US Marines guarding the Arraijan fuel tank farm north-west of Howard AFB foiled one of several attempted penetrations when intruders tripped a warning flare. The incident was hushed up, as the intruders were actually some 50

16th MP Bde. (Abn) MPs load PDF prisoners aboard US Balboa school buses for transport to a holding compound. The MP at the far left is armed with a 12 ga. Remington M870 MKI riot shotgun. (DoD)

Rangers aboard a specially modified 'gun jeep' 1/4-ton M151A2 utility truck fitted with two M60 machine guns, equipment boxes, and roll bars. (DoD)

Cuban Ministry of Interior Special Troops (*Trupas Especial de Ministerio del Interior*); their one dead and seven wounded were taken to a PDF hospital and spirited out of the country the next night. This was one of the more serious of many examples of Cuban meddling in Panama. It was also during this period that the flow of Cuban arms into the country increased, usually flown in by PDF aircraft. Noriega also permitted the Cuban Directorate General of Intelligence (*Directorate Generál de Inteligencia*—DGI) to operate a communications intercept station in the jungle. Harassment, provocations, arrests, and threats involving US citizens increased, with 240 incidents reported in 1988.

At the beginning of 1989 the various opposition parties united in an effort to counter Noriega's front party, the National Liberation Coalition. The Civic Opposition Democratic Alliance ran Guillermo Endara for president; and despite Noriega's best efforts to rig the May 1989 elections, Endara won by a landslide. While outside observers exposed Noriega's attempted election fraud, 'Dignity Battalion' thugs were seen on world-wide television beating opposition leaders in the streets with iron bars. Noriega simply declared the elections null and void before the results were released. The Organization of American States (OAS) convened a special meeting, but were reluctant to intervene in a member state's affairs; despite months of deliberation no action was taken.

PDF incidents involving US troops and dependents increased, ranging from petty harassment to sexual threats and severe beatings. A handful of US citizens were arrested and imprisoned on spy charges, without the notification of US authorities. Panamanian opposition members were also arrested without cause, some not to be seen again until mass graves were uncovered after 'Just Cause'. In one March incident PDF troops detained school buses carrying the children of American military dependents in Balboa; US MPs arrived at the scene just as the PDF began to take the children into custody, quickly announcing that the first PDF stepping toward the buses would be shot. In another incident a group of PDF were caught stealing a 105 mm howitzer from Ft. Sherman.

President George Bush deployed additional troops as part of Operation 'Nimrod Dancer', and many of the 14,000 military dependents and 8,400 US civilian military employees were returned to the States. The US stressed that it would honour the 1978 treaty to turn the Canal over to Panama, though Noriega still insisted his actions were motivated by the US's desire to abrogate the treaty. Public services almost came to a standstill when unpaid workers refused to report in, and the PDF took over operation of many of these.

The October 1989 coup

As the situation deteriorated a desperate group of PDF officers attempted another coup on 3 Oct. 1989, President Bush having openly invited such an action. Led by Maj. Moisés Giroldi, commanding the 4th Inf. Co., the fewer than 300 rebels actually succeeded in capturing Noriega in *La Comandancía*; however, rather than arresting or simply killing the dictator, they attempted to persuade him to retire peacefully. The commander of the supposedly loyal Bn. 2000 had initially planned to aid the rebels, but co-ordination was faulty and he waited two hours before deploying. By this time the 1st Inf. Combat and Fire Spt. Co. had flown from Rio Hato, by-passing US roadblocks. Bn. 2000 then turned on the rebels. US officials were ill-prepared for such an eventuality and efforts to aid the rebellion were ineffective. US roadblocks were able to prevent the 5th Inf. Co. deploying from Ft. Amador and delayed the loyal 7th Inf. Co. on the Bridge of the Americas over the Canal, but this had little overall effect. The coup failed miserably, with considerable embarrassment to the US government, though it was felt that direct US participation would have discredited the opposition and angered other Latin American states. Noriega, waving a machete on television, declared a 'victory' over the *Yanquis*, and was reported to have personally tortured and shot the coup leader; other plotters met a similar fate, including some of Noriega's trusted inner circle. The resulting purge strained the loyalty of many PDF personnel, and Noriega now trusted even fewer. He even required his mistress's mother to prepare his meals as protection from poisoning.

At the beginning of September 1989 Noriega had appointed a provisional president, Francisco Rodriguez, but retained actual control of the government. On 15 Dec. Noriega took a course of action that no sovereign state could tolerate: he pressured the legislature into declaring that a state of war existed with the USA. At the same time he was appointed the 'Maximum Leader' and chief executive officer of the government to respond to 'US war actions'. US treaty verification officers were forced to accompany convoys to ensure that rights of access were permitted by the PDF, which often established roadblocks on otherwise open roads. During this period the PDF and US forces maintained constant surveillance on each other's activities, facilities, and troop movements. The US made special efforts to keep track of Noriega's whereabouts. Harassment of US personnel continued, and on 16 Dec. the worst happened. Four US Marine officers in civilian clothes became lost, drove by *La Comandancía*, and were fired on when they refused to stop at a roadblock; a lieutenant was killed by PDF gunfire. A US Navy officer and his wife walking in the area witnessed the shooting and were detained by PDF personnel; the officer was beaten and his wife threatened with rape, a common PDF harassment tactic. The next day President Bush directed the execution of Operation 'Just Cause'. On 18 Dec. a US Army officer wounded a Panamanian police officer when he thought the policeman was about to pull a gun on him. It was reported through informers that Noriega had laid plans to attack American neighborhoods and schools.

US forces were ordered to protect US lives and facilities to apprehend Noriega and deliver him to competent authority, to neutralize PDF forces, to support the establishment of a US-recognized government, and to restructure the PDF.

Maj. Gen. James H. Johnson, Jr., commanding the 82d Abn. Div., confers with the 1/75th Rangers staff. (DoD)

JUST CAUSE

The world awoke on the morning of 20 Dec. 1989 to the stunning news that US armed forces had invaded Panama. Most key objectives were secured and organized resistance was eliminated by mid-morning. Once the order for execution had been given on 17 Dec. events unfolded at a rapid tempo, and in less than 60 hours parachutes blossomed over Panama.

In the States the units were alerted that same night, a Sunday. On Monday morning the troops received their orders, began load-out, and were ready to launch within 24 hours. The 82d Abn. Div.'s reinforced 1st Bde. conducted a mass jump rehearsal on Sicily Drop Zone replicating the Tocumén/Torrijos Airports, and soon departed Pope AFB despite a 28 degree ice storm; six hours away Panama was sweltering in 91 degrees. The 75th Ranger Regt., launching from bases in Georgia, were scheduled to arrive just before the 82d's battalions; the Rangers had had the benefit of conducting rehearsals during 9–16 December. The 2d Bde., 7th Inf. Div. (Lt) departed from Travis AFB, Calif., with some flights delayed by fog, and arrived on the heels of the 82d after a nine-hour flight. Dozens of other units marshalled to await their turn in the aerial pipeline. The deposed President Guillermo Endara was sworn in on the evening of 19 Dec. and was operating from the legislative assembly building by 21 December.

In Panama the commanders in the 193d Inf. Bde. (Lt) (Sep), in-place units of the 3d Bde. (−), 7th Inf. and 82d Abn. Divs., and the Marines were informed of the operation at 1900 hours on 19 December. The troops were briefed at 2100 hours, and soon began deploying in a pattern they had often rehearsed under the guise of the 'Sand Flea' freedom of movement exercises. Carefully concealed combat multipliers, covertly deployed to Panama earlier, emerged from their hangars at Howard AFB; these were the Sheridan tanks and AH-64 Apache and AH-6 gunships. Air Force AC-130 gunships, joined by a flight of five arriving directly from Florida, began prowling the skies over Panama City, using their array of night vision equipment and sensors to confirm PDF dispositions.

The PDF commander at Rio Hato, not having been told otherwise, had given some of his troops Christmas leave. Most of the PDF slumbered in their far-flung dispersal areas. The increasing US activity, as in-place units began their initial deployments, did tip off some PDF commanders up to two hours prior to H-Hour. Noriega was in bed with a prostitute at the *La Siesta* Officers' Club on Tocumén Air Base after spending the day in Coco Solo. Though notified shortly before H-Hour he

Members of the 75th Ranger Regt. establish a company command post *among civilian spectators. (75th Ranger Regt.)*

of the ordinary was afoot. (It
, ranging from the US State
may have tipped Noriega off,
timely or effective manner.)
n to descend on the air base.
ost of the time hiding out at
ary. He never attempted to
tile defense, nor communi-
as his personal safety.
or the use of overwhelming forces
, moderately armed, comparatively poorly
prepared force. This accusation is unfounded for
ons. There are simply too many unknowns in warfare.
Any commander who, by choice, leads into offensive combat a
force of only marginally more strength than his opponent is
assuming an unwarranted risk. If certain aspects of the operation
go amiss, sufficient combat power may not be available to effect a
favorable outcome, at least in some areas. Friendly troops would
be placed in unnecessary danger, certain phases of the mission
would be delayed, and other locally available units would have to
be redirected (thus even further disrupting the operation plan) or
additional external forces would have to be committed. The
second reason concerns securing cleared areas. While a smaller
force could have easily defeated the PDF in a set-piece battle, it
was fully realized that the enemy would not choose to fight in this
manner. There was a real danger of PDF infiltration into the

cleared areas and of 'stay-behind' resistance. The US would have
to secure these areas along with their vulnerable lines of
communications, military facilities, key terrain and installations,
and dependent housing areas (all widely scattered), as well as
protecting Panamanians from the expected looters and roving
Dig Bat bands. All of this had to be accomplished in sprawling
metropolitan areas at night. As it was, the personnel of many antiarmor, mortar, artillery, and other units were pressed into
security rôles. These security missions in the cities became even
more critical, especially since there were no civil police to
maintain order, when many of the maneuver battalions spread
out into the countryside to search for PDF renegades and to
disarm garrisons. The main fear was not of organized resistance,
but of small harassing attacks, sniping, and banditry against the
populace. No attempt was made by the PDF to attack any Canal
facilities, but it was closed for 29 hours (20 Dec.)—the first time
since its opening.

Operation 'Just Cause' bore the trademark of Gen. Colin L.
Powell, the Chairman of the Joint Chiefs of Staff: go in quick with

2.75-inch rocket strikes are evident on a 16-story apartment building adjacent to La Comandancia and occupied by the PDF. They brought fire down on Task Force Gator troops as they assaulted the PDF headquarters, until suppressed by AH-6 and AH-64 attack helicopters. (DoD)

overwhelming combat power; make maximum use of all armed services' unique capabilities; and withdraw when the mission is accomplished, leaving only those necessary to aid civil authorities with stability operations and nation-building.

Rather than attempt to follow the confusing hour-by-hour sequence of events, we will discuss each of the major task forces' specific operations.

Task Force Red

TF Red was tasked with two widely separated missions. The first was to secure the Rio Hato Military Base (55 miles west of Panama City), defended by an estimated 720 heavily armed PDF. TF Red Romeo was composed of a 75th Ranger Regt. command and control element (Team Black); 2d Bn., 75th Rangers; 3d Bn. (−Co. C), 75th Rangers; three 1st Psyops. Bn. loudspeaker teams; and an aviation element with AH-6 and AH-64 gunships. An AC-130 gunship provided additional fire support. The 2/75 Rangers had previously deployed from Ft. Lewis, Wash., to Ft. Benning, Ga., to conduct rehearsals with 3/75. Departing Ft.

Benning's Lawson Army Air
13 C-130s, the TF was precede
Each dropped a 2000-lb. bomb
in fact this only served to al
Rangers with small arms and
hours, 20 Dec., the Rangers ju
east of the main runway; a stiff
injuries. (Normal peacetime tr
feet, though the Rangers mac
Federal Aviation Administratic

The 2/75 immediately assau
Cos.' barracks and the Militar
the base HQ, communicatio
blocked the nearby Inter-An
secure, the first transport land
2/75 was then ordered to seize
at Farallon. The Rangers los
Battalions' Cos. A and B), 27
Rio Hato. PDF losses were 34
with 16 armoured vehicles, 11 2
Much of two of Noriega's r
neutralized, and the US now
Panama City to support future

TF Red Tango was com
command and control eleme
reinforced by C/3/75, three 1s

The exterior of the white-painted main headquarters building of La Comandancia,
breached by M551A1 Sheridan tank 152 mm guns. (Maj. B. A. Kilgariff)

and a team from the 96th CA Bn., supported by AH-6 attack helicopters and an AC-130 gunship. The TF was tasked with neutralizing the 2d Abn. Inf. Co. and securing the Tocumén/Torrijos Airports for the 82d Abn. Div.'s follow-on insertion. Flying out of Hunter Army Air Field, Ga., the force was preceded by 15 minutes by a heavy equipment drop, with all four companies jumping directly on to the fields from 500 ft. at 0110 hours. While 1/75 cleared the 2d Inf. Abn. Co.'s positions, C/3/75 seized the main terminal. The upper two floors were quickly secured, but PDF troops had barricaded themselves on the first floor with 347 Brazilian hostages from a late arriving flight. In just over an hour the TF had secured all objectives with the exception of the hostage situation. With the aid of psyops. loudspeaker teams, a peaceful resolution of the situation was agreed after two and a half hours of negotiating. The first transports were able to land by 0900 hours. The 1/75 came under the operational control of the 82d Abn. Div. by late morning. Friendly casualties were one dead (HHC), five wounded, and 19 jump injuries (Jump injuries were excessive due to most troops landing on the runways, and included sprained or twisted knees and ankles and some fractures. Typically, battalion jumps at night with full combat equipment yield only two or three injuries.) PDF losses were 13 dead, 54 prisoners plus several recoilless rifles and 13 fixed wing aircraft.

The Rangers went on to execute a number of follow-on missions. The 1/75 conducted a reconnaissance in force to Cerro Azul to pursue renegade PDF; it was redeployed to Hunter Army Air Field on 3 Jan. to be available for any other worldwide contingency missions should the need arise. C/3/75 was placed in TF reserve and then sent to aid with securing *La Comandancia*. Later on the 20th A/2/75 was flown to Panama City to relieve the hard-hit SEALs at Paitilla Airport, remaining there until the 27th. C/3/75, relieved from *La Comandancia*, was sent to reinforce the US Embassy until the 28th. Elements of 3/75 were deployed to Penonome during 21–23 Dec., and other elements

Originally painted matt black, the 2d Anti-riot Co.s' two burned-out Mercedes-Benz water cannon trucks rest inside La Comandancia. They were known as 'Smurf Mobiles', or 'Pitufo' to Panamanians, due to the blue Smurf cartoon characters painted on their sides. (Maj. B. A. Kilgariff)

were dispatched to David between 22 and 26 December. C/2/75 was deployed to Nueva Guarrare during 23–24 December. The 2d and 3d Bns. were then tasked with security operations, until they stood down on 7 Jan. and returned to home stations on 9–10 Jan. The Rangers captured over 1,000 PDF and Dig Bat personnel and confiscated almost 16,000 weapons.

Task Force Pacific

The 1st Bde. (+), 82d Abn. Div., the Division Ready Brigade, was comprised of its 1st and 2d Bns., 504th Parachute Inf. Regt.; the 4th Bn., 325th Abn. Inf. Regt. and Co. A, 3-505th Parachute Inf. Regt. (the battalion's only company to deploy). The Brigade's 3-504 was already in-place in Panama attached to 3d Bde. (−), 7th Inf. Division. Supporting the Brigade were the 82d's Assault Command Post plus elements of the 3d Bn. (105 mm Towed) (Abn), 319th FA Regt., and Co. C (−), 3d Bn. (Lt) (Abn), 73d Armor Regiment. The Brigade was to parachute on to Torrijos Airport and then conduct a number of air assaults flown by UH-60As of the in-place TF Hawk. Other 82d units (most arriving later) included elements of the 82d Signal, 30th Combat Engr., and 313th MI Bns. plus Co. B, 307th Medical; Co. A, 407th Supply and Trans.; Co. A, 782d Maint. Bns.; and Bty. A, 3d Bn., 4th ADA Regt., along with some XVIII Abn. Corps elements. Though the field was secure, the Brigade jumped in so as to get on the ground quickly and prevent air and runway traffic jams.

At 2130 hours, 19 Dec., the first of 20 C-141 transports loaded with 2,200 troops and tons of equipment lifted out of Pope AFB. All equipment and personnel were to have been dropped in one pass, but due to the ice storm causing the delay of many aircraft they arrived in three waves. Over the airport the lead C-141s received ground fire, wounding one trooper. About 50 jump injuries were sustained, but like many of the injured Rangers the paratroopers often refused evacuation and continued on with their units. A small part of the force was mis-dropped south and east of the airport, landing among the swamps and trees, which delayed some units' assembly. Dropped in with this force were eight Sheridan tanks, the first time they were para-dropped in an actual combat operation. Two were attached to each battalion and the fourth pair to a force blocking the airport's entrance.

The first unit out the door over Torrijos was 2-504 at 0210 hours. At 0600 hours the battalion was air-assaulted into Panamá La Viejo on the Pacific coast, while the unit's Co. D and two Sheridan tanks drove from the airport to link up with the force. They encountered a strong roadblock and two more Sheridans were dispatched. Of the two landing zones, both were under fire and the one along the beach turned out to be a mud flat. Helicopter crews hovered under fire to pull out paratroopers mired armpit deep in mud while Panamanian civilians formed a human chain, under fire, to pull out more.

The PDF's Cav. Sdn. and the Special Security Antiterrorist Unit had been alerted and put up a stiff fight, but the objective was secured by 1200 hours. Through the afternoon car-loads of

PDF and Dig Bats arrived at the battalion's position and opened fire. Most of these were destroyed, along with four V-300 armored cars. In the afternoon Co. B, fighting off attacks along the way, moved to secure the Marriott Hotel where a number of US news media personnel were in danger of being taken hostage. After the hotel was secured 29 US citizens were escorted back to Panamá La Viejo and flown out the next day. The unit's Co. D lost one man.

The 1-504 was the next into Torrijos Airport. At 0830 the battalion air-assaulted into Tinajitas to neutralize the 1st Inf. Combat and Fire Spt. Company. Receiving ground fire en route, they drew more of the same while landing at the objective. The paratroopers fought their way up 400 meters of hillside to the objective against heavy small arms and mortar fire. A house-to-house fight ensued, with the objective not secured until 1430 hours. The next day was spent clearing the surrounding area of snipers and later conducting security operations. The battalion's HHC and Co. B each lost a man.

The 4-325 was the last into Torrijos at 0500. At 1000 hours A/4-325 executed an air assault into Ft. Cimarrón to clear the remnants of Bn. 2000, followed by Co. C. Co. C secured the airport while Co. D was dispatched to reinforce the SEALs at Paitilla Airport. AC-130 gunships had knocked out most of Bn. 2000's armored vehicles and they further shot up the garrison. Meeting only light resistance, Co. A found that most of the élite unit had melted away leaving 13 dead, ten destroyed armored vehicles, and three 120 mm mortars. The remainder of the battalion arrived on 22 December. The battalion was later tasked with security around the Papal Nunciatura where Noriega had taken refuge. The 4-325 HHC lost one man.

Panamanians line up for registration by US MPs, Panama City. Some came to turn in recovered weapons for $150 cash each. (Maj. B. A. Kilgariff)

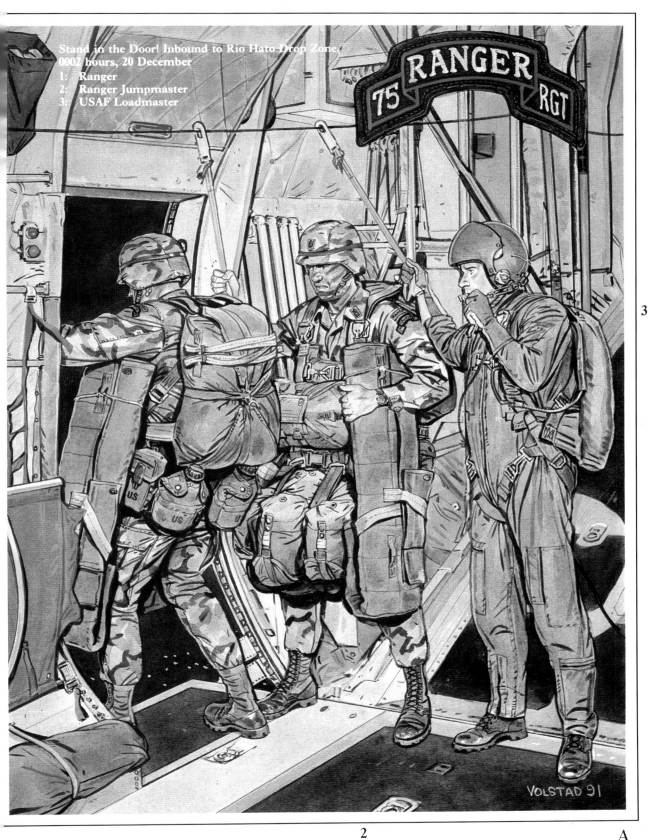

Stand in the Door! Inbound to Rio Hato Drop Zone,
0002 hours, 20 December
1: Ranger
2: Ranger Jumpmaster
3: USAF Loadmaster

VOLSTAD 91

A

The 'Maximum Leader'

B

Noriega's 'Boots'
1: Panamanian Police Force officer
2: Police Force 2nd Anti-riot Co. officer
3: Special Security Anti-terrorist Unit soldier
4: Dignity Battalion member

VOLSTAD91

C

1: Mortarman, 1st Bde., 82nd Abn. Division
2: Grenadier, 5-87th Inf., 193d Inf. Brigade
3: Radio/Telephone Operator, 4-6th Inf., 5th Inf. Division

D

VOLSTAD 91

1: SAW Gunner, 2nd Bde., 7th Inf.
   Division
2: Sniper, 1st Bde., 7th Inf. Division

3: Tactical Air Control Party
   member, Det. 5, 602d Tactical Air
   Control Wing, 7th Inf. Division
4: Air Liaison Officer, Det. 5, 602d
   Tactical Air Control Wing, 7th Inf.
   Division

1: 'Delta Force' Assault Team operator
2: Special Forces trooper, A/3/7th SFGA
3: Navy SEAL Team 4 member

VOLSTAD 91

F

VOLSTAD 91

AIRBORNE

1: **Military Policeman, 401st MP Co., 89th MP Brigade**
2: **Military Policeman, 108th MPCo., 16th MP Bde.**
    (Airborne)
3: **MP Humvee**
4: **Light truck driver, A/193d Forward Spt. Battalion**

VOLSTAD 91

1: LAV-25 Light Armored Vehicle, D/2d LAI Battalion
2: LAV-25 vehicle commander, D/2d LAI Battalion
3: 1st Fleet Antiterrorist Security Team Plt. member
4: SMAW Gunner, K/3/6th Marines

H

PDF uniforms
1:   1st Inf. Combat and Fire Spt. Co. 'Tigre'

2:   2d Inf. Abn. Co. 'Puma'
3:   3d Inf. Co. 'Diablo Rojo'
4:   5th Inf. Co., MP Bn. 'Victoriano Lorenzo'
5:   Co. A 'Fortuna', 2d Bn. 'Paz'

1: PDF V-150 APC, 6th Mech. Inf. Company
2: PDF V-300 Fire Support Vehicle, Bn. 2000

J

'La Noche de Fuego' (The Night of Fire); Inside
La Comandancia
1: 6th Mech. Inf. Company
2: 7th Inf. Co. 'Macho de Monte.'
3: Maneuver Co. 'Furia' Bn. 2000

2

3

K

1: **US Army UH-60A aviator, 1-288th Aviation**
2: **USAF OF-37B pilot, 24th Tactical Spt. Squadron**
3: **USAF AC-130H Gunner, 16th Special Ops. Squadron**

VOLSTAD 91

L

From 22 Dec. all three battalions conducted stability operations until relieved by units of the 7th Inf. Div. on 10 January. On 22 Dec. PDF 'hold-outs' staged limited mortar attacks against USSOUTHCOM HQ on Quarry Heights and Albrook AFB. The news media immediately questioned the Army's ability to protect itself, though there is no way to prevent long-range indirect fire attacks. Hard core PDF also attempted to assassinate the new Panamanian first vice-president. Between 10 and 12 Jan. the 1st Bde. and other 82d Abn. Div. elements redeployed to Ft. Bragg, most (2,000) of them jumping in to be greeted by thousands of cheering families and local well-wishers.

The bulk of the 7th Inf. Div. (Lt) arrived between 20 and 22 Dec. and was initially placed under the operational control of the 82d Abn. Division. Deploying with the Division were elements of its 7th Supply and Trans., 7th Medical, 13th Combat Engr., 127th Signal, 307th MI, and 707th Maint. Bns., and 7th MP and 536th Aircraft Maint. Cos. plus other units. Once deployed, the Division HQ was located in Panama City and the logistics operated out of Howard AFB.

The first element to arrive was the 2d Bde. comprised of 5th Bn., 21st Inf.; 2d and 3d Bns., 27th Inf.; and 7th Bn. (105 mm Towed), 15th FA Regt. (— one battery). Airlanded by C-141s at Torrijos Airport at 1200 hours, 20 Dec., the Brigade took up security positions until the next day. Assigned a huge area of operations from west of Panama City to the Costa Rican border, the Brigade's first missions included air-assaulting 5-21 into Coclecio on 22 Dec., while 2-27 and 3-27 relieved the Rangers of TF Red Romeo at Rio Hato and the Brigade HQ established there. On 22 Dec. 800 troops of the PDF's 2d Bn. and 7th Inf. Co. surrendered at David along with hundreds of support and FP personnel. (It had been feared that this force in Chiriqui Province, a notorious Noriega stronghold, would pursue a guerrilla war in the jungles.) B/3-27 air-assaulted into Las Tablas where it took 200 prisoners. The 5-21 then relocated to David to relieve 3/75 Rangers, where it remained until relieved by 2d and 3d Bns., 7th SFGA on 8 January. The Brigade then moved to Panama City to relieve the 1st Bde., 82d Abn. Div.; here it conducted stability operations, becoming responsible for the entire area on 13 January. Part of 2-27 was deployed to David to demonstrate the US's ability to rapidly inject a force into any part of the country in support of the new government. Next the Brigade expanded its operations east from Panama City. Between 24 Jan. and 6 Feb. it demonstrated a strong US presence in support of the new government, and searched for PDF renegades. On 6 Feb. the 2d Bde. began redeployment to Ft. Ord.

The 1st Bde., 7th Inf. Div. was alerted on 20 Dec. for deployment to Panama. Comprising the 1st, 2d and 3d Bns., 9th Inf. Regt., the Brigade often refers to itself as the 9th Regimental Combat Team. The unit had operated out of Ft. Sherman during Operation 'Nimrod Dancer' from May to Oct. 1989 when relieved by the 3d Brigade. The Brigade, initially attached to the 82d, was now tasked with securing much of Panama City. The first elements of 3-9 Inf. landed at Howard AFB on 22 Dec. and in 12 hours were engaged in rooting out snipers. All Brigade elements arrived by 24 Dec., and they too were sent into the city, where 21 engagements were fought with PDF and Dig Bat elements. The Brigade was also responsible for securing the US Embassy and the new government's offices plus many other key facilities. It also blocked off the Cuban, Nicaraguan, and Libyan Embassies to prevent Noriega and his henchmen from seeking asylum. On 6 Jan. it took over the security of the Papal Nunciatura where Noriega had gained sanctuary. On 10 Jan. the

Brigade was relieved from the 82d and placed under the 7th Inf. Div.'s control, where it assumed an even larger area of responsibility from the departing 82d. The units manned roadblocks and conducted countless patrols to protect against looters. The 3-9 was also responsible for conducting initial training of the new Panama Public Force (PPF) in order to field a replacement for the Police Force. On 17 Jan. the 1st Bde. turned over its area to the 2d Bde. and combined US MP/PPF control, and returned to Ft. Ord between 17 and 22 January.

Elements of 6-8 FA returned to Ft. Ord on 2 Jan., being the first 7th Inf. Div. unit to do so. The other artillery units, after accomplishing their initial fire support missions, were principally tasked with security duties. On 31 Jan. 4-21 deployed to Panama to relieve 5-21 Infantry.

Task Force Atlantic

The 3d Bde. (—), 7th Inf. Div. arrived in Panama on 15 Oct. to relieve the 1st Bde., which returned to Ft. Ord, in the Colón area. Dubbed TF Atlantic, the Brigade controlled 4th Bn., 17th Inf. and 3d Bn., 504th Parachute Inf. Regt. (82d Abn. Div.) plus MP units. The preceding weeks saw the TF rotating its battalions through the Jungle Operations Training Center (JOTC), conducting 'Sand Flea' freedom of movement convoys between Forts Sherman and Clayton and Howard AFB on the far side of the isthmus, and rehearsing its part of OPLAN 90-2.

At 0038 hours, 20 Dec., the units deployed to secure a variety of objectives. C/4-17 attacked the PDF 1st Naval Inf. Co. at Coco Solo, and Co. A the 8th Inf. Co. at Ft. Espinar. Other elements established roadblocks at the neck of the Colón peninsula and Boyd-Roosevelt Highway, secured the Galeta Island facility and dependent housing areas, and disabled PDF aircraft at France Airfield. The A/4-17 met stiff resistance from the 8th Inf. Co., and it took direct artillery fire from the 7-15 FA and the total destruction of the barracks before the base was secured and 90 prisoners taken. Ft. Sherman and the Gatun Locks were secured by the JOTC cadre.

One of the most critical of these missions fell to C/4-17: neutralizing the 1st Naval Inf. Co. located at Coco Solo across the Canal from Cristóbal. A small US housing area was only 50 meters from the PDF unit's compound, from which they had harassed dependents. The company was reinforced by a platoon each from 3-504 Inf. and 549th MP Co. The force's assault element, Co. C's 2d Plt., attacked with the support of two 2d Bn., 62d ADA 20 mm Vulcan guns while the remainder of the force surrounded the compound. It took four hours to clear it, but the small assault force did not suffer even a single injury and managed to take 38 prisoners.

The 3-504 was tasked with securing the Madden Dam (critical to the Canal's operation), the PDF's Cerro Tigre supply base, the town of Gamboa, and Gamboa and Renacer Prisons. A specially rehearsed force centered on C/3-504 was given the mission of taking the Renacer Prison. The execution of this precision mission demonstrated a level of skill normally expected of SF and Ranger units. Attacking at 0100 hours, two 1st Bn., 228th Avn. Regt. UH-1Hs bearing two squads landed inside the prison compound, while an AH-1S Cobra attacked the guards' barracks and two OH-58Cs fired on guard posts. Other company elements landed from two 1097th Trans. Co. LCM landing craft. Another UH-1H landed a team outside the compound to block any PDF reinforcements. Despite the complexity of the mission and the close proximity of the engagements on a moonless night, the US

A Marine 1st FAST Plt. member searches for PDF 'hold-outs' in Arrijan. He is armed with a 9 mm Colt M16 sub-machine gun and M9 pistol in a special thigh holster. Note the special M16 leg magazine pouches. (DoD)

16th MP Bde. (Abn) M1025 armament carrier HMWVVs, mounting M60 machine guns, patrol the streets of Panama City. (Maj. B. A. Kilgariff)

orce suffered only four wounded while killing five PDF guards nd taking 22 PDF prisoners, all without injuring a single prison nmate.

Another 3-504 element was targeted on the Gamboa Prison where coup attempt prisoners and a CIA agent were held. nserted by helicopters, the attack was lightning fast and all 48 risoners were liberated. All of TF Atlantic's missions had been uccessfully accomplished by 0600 hours.

The TF then entered Colón on 22 Dec., delayed due to the uge numbers of prisoners who were surrendering at 4-17's oadblock outside the city, though numerous 'hold-outs' were till dug in. The 4-17 conducted an amphibious assault into the ity's Duty Free Zone and advanced into the eastern part while wo 3-504 companies entered from the south through Cristóbal upported by elements of 7-15 FA. Resistance was light and arious PDF installations were quickly secured, along with 400 risoners. TF Atlantic quickly became engaged in civil military perations, i.e. re-establishing law and order and assisting with ebuilding (this included repairing the sewer system and hospital,

and distributing food). On 4 Jan. elements of the Brigade returned to Forts Sherman and Espinar, and Coco Solo. The 3-504 redeployed to Ft. Bragg on 6 Jan., the first 82d unit to do so. The 4-17 was relieved by the just-arriving 3-17 on 16 Jan. and returned to Ft. Ord on 22 January. C/4-17 had lost one man.

TF Bayonet

The 193d Inf. Bde. (Lt) (Sep) was the only combat unit normally assigned to US Army, South, having been stationed there since 1952. With only two assigned maneuver battalions, 5th Bn. (Lt), 87th and 1st Bn. (Abn), 508th Inf. Regts., it was augmented during Operation 'Nimrod Sustain' by 4th Bn. (Mech), 6th Inf. Regt. and Trp. D (Air), 3d Sdn., 1st Cav. Regt. (both detached from 5th Inf. Div. (Mech) at Ft. Polk, La.), plus US Army, South's 92d MP Bn. (Provisional). The Brigade was also assigned Bty. D (105 mm Towed), 320th FA Regt.; 193d Forward Spt. Bn.; 193d MI Co.; 396th Signal Co.; and 518th Engr. Co. (Combat). The Brigade is headquartered at Ft. Clayton with

elements at Forts Knobbe and Sherman. Having conducted extensive rehearsals, the Brigade's three battalion task forces were each given three missions, all particularly demanding due to the expected resistance.

TF Gator was composed of 4-6 Inf. (−Co. A), C/1-508 Inf., and Team Armor. This latter small force comprised the 82d Abn. Div.'s 3d Plt., Co. C, 1st Bn., 73d Armor with four Sheridans, and the Marines' 2d Plt., Co. D, 2d Lt. Armd. Inf. Bn. with four LAV-25s. Its mission was to attack and secure the well-defended *La Comandancia*. H-Hour, set for 0100, was advanced 15 minutes when some PDF outside Howard AFB became aware that US troops were beginning to deploy and began firing into the base. The force immediately received heavy fire when the assault began. Two of the lead platoon's M113A3 APCs were hit by RPGs, and casualties quickly mounted; B/4-6 and C/1-508 each lost a man and suffered large numbers of wounded. Despite this, *La Comandancia* was isolated by 0330. A massive amount of fire was poured into the complex from machine guns, LAWs, mortars, Sheridan 152 mm guns, LAV 25 mm cannons, attack helicopter machine guns and 30 mm cannons, and AC-130's 20, 40 and 105 mm guns. Though this turned much of it into an inferno, the hard core PDF continued to hold out, returning fire from the complex and surrounding buildings. A desperate break-out attempt was cut to pieces. C/3/75 Rangers were sent to reinforce TF Gator and tasked to clear the main HQ building while C/1-508 was to clear the remainder of the complex. The

final bitter assault was launched at 1600 hours, when the wall was breached by two 40 lb. cratering charges; and the objective was secured at 1730 with the PDF suffering extensive casualties. Part of TF Gator was then dispatched to the US Embassy, which was under attack, and secured it until relieved by Rangers. Follow-on missions included securing the Papal Nunciatura and various US facilities in Panama City. The TF was relieved on 22 Jan. by 3-6 Inf. fresh from Ft. Polk.

TF Wildcat was composed of 5-87 Inf. reinforced by the APC-mounted A/4-6 Infantry. The TF attacked and secured several PDF and FP facilities in Balboa, accomplishing these missions by 0700, and helping to isolate *La Comandancia*. The TF spent the rest of the operation securing a number of areas in Panama City and conducting civil military operations.

TF Red Devil consisted of 1-508 Inf. (−Co. C). The battalion was originally to air-assault into Ft. Amador to engage the 5th Inf. Co.; however, since H-Hour was moved up 15 minutes, two platoons moved by truck to block the main gate as the helicopters were not ready. Two bus loads of PDF attempted to break out and one was destroyed. The rest of the TF air-assaulted in at 0100 as planned, and found themselves under heavy fire. Regardless, by 0130 the barracks were surrounded and the US dependent housing area secured. A loudspeaker team announced surrender terms which the PDF chose to ignore. The TF assaulted at sunrise, meeting stiff resistance, with the HHC losing one man. The barracks was not secured until 1645—the last PDF

Marine LAV-25 of Co. D/2d LAI Bn. patrols the town of Arrijan on 20 Dec. 1989. A 50-foot coil of concertina razor wire is secured on the deck forward of the turret. (DoD)

A Marine sniper of the 1st FAST Plt., attached D/2d LAI Bn., checks out a suspicious person in Arrijan with a scope-mounted M16A2 rifle. (DoD)

A Black Hawk UH-60A helicopter of 2-123d Avn. Regt., 7th Inf. Div. is off-loaded from a C-5A Galaxy transport at Howard AFB. US Army

helicopters are painted with infrared-absorbent matt dark olive green paint and are not camouflaged. (DoD)

installation to fall—with 141 prisoners taken. The remainder of the operation saw the TF conducting various security and civil military tasks throughout Panama City.

Joint Special Ops. Task Force

Special operations forces were controlled by the JSOTF, whose headquarters was provided by Special Operations Command, South (SOCSOUTH), a small joint planning and co-ordinating staff subordinate to USSOUTHCOM. Subordinate to it were the 3d Bn. (+), 7th SFGA; 75th Ranger Regt.; the SEALs; 'Delta Force'; TF 160; and 528th Spt. Bn. (Airborne).

The 3d Bn., 7th SFGA, based at Ft. Davis, had been in Panama since replacing the 8th SFGA in 1972. The TF was augmented by A/1/7 SFGA from Ft. Bragg. The force was tasked with a wide variety of specialized missions; while many of these were appropriate for SF, others were not. One of the nagging fears of any special ops. soldier is misuse by higher conventional forces headquarters; however, in this instance some overzealous SF officers sought conventional missions from higher headquarters in order to get a piece of the action. Missions prior to 20 Dec. had focused on intelligence collection, surveillance of the PDF, and drop zone reconnaissance, as well as keeping tabs on Noriega's movements (he changed residences up to four times a night). On D-Day specially trained elements of 3/7 SF raided the

TV2 station at Cerro Azul, two government-operated radio stations, and several locations frequented by Noriega. The TV2 raid is of particular interest in that the team simply removed certain critical transmitter components and departed. Later the components were re-installed and the station turned over to the new government, allowing it to broadcast information to the people and surrender instructions to stubborn PDF and Dig Bat elements. Special Operations Command and Control Elements (SOCCE), provided by B-Teams, were co-located with all conventional brigades and proved invaluable for co-ordination in often confused tactical situations, to prevent 'blue-on-blue' engagements and provide advice on SF capabilities. A small 3/7 SF element secured Ft. Davis.

A tactical mission in direct support of conventional forces— not exactly SF's customary rôle, but none the less critical—was to seize the Pacora River Bridge about 15 km north-east of the Torrijos/Tocumén Airport. Securing it would block any reinforcement by Bn. 2000 at Ft. Cimarrón only 4 km away. Twenty-two men of A/3/7 SF were inserted by three UH-60As at 0045 hours on 20 Dec., their H-Hour had been moved up as had those of other units, and they received fire as they lifted off from Albrook AFB. On landing the SF troopers discovered the lead elements of a large Bn. 2000 convoy already approaching the bridge. Three M136 LAW-armed troopers rushed into the road and fired on the lead vehicles, blocking the following convoy on the elevated highway. As an AC-130H picked off armored vehicles lined up on the road the SF troopers brought heavy fire to bear on the dismounting PDF. With virtually every vehicle destroyed in this, Bn. 2000's only attempt to deploy, the remnants melted away. The situation was stabilized by 0130 hours and the small force was reinforced at 0600. US intelligence was uncertain of the élite battalion's status and expected it to strike elsewhere, but it never did.

Beginning on 2 Jan., TF Black's follow-on missions were less spectacular. The remainder of the 7th SFGA had arrived from Ft. Bragg on 30 Dec. to assist with these operations. Some elements, in conjunction with SEALs in TFs Blue and Green, were tasked with searching various PDF headquarters and Noriega's houses and other haunts. Most SF units were deployed to the outlying provinces to neutralize PDF garrisons and gain control of the military zone HQs for the new government. This was usually accomplished by flying an SF company into the town's local airfield, from where the SF commander telephoned the PDF garrison commander and asked him to meet him at the airport to discuss surrender terms (most 3/7 SF personnel speak Spanish). The terms were simple: (1) unconditional surrender, (2) place all weapons in the arms room, and (3) form the garrison on the parade ground. The SF searched the compound and processed the PDF troops. A standby 7th Inf. Div. rifle company would then fly in and take charge of the garrison, establish law and order in the town, and prevent looting and reprisals on the PDF by civilians. An SF A-Team remained with the rifle company to provide linguistic support and to begin providing medical aid and other assistance to the locals. This method was successful and no casualties were suffered by either side while accepting the surrender of garrisons.

Most of the 7th SFGA redeployed to Ft. Bragg at the end of January. The 3/7 SF, after so lengthy a tour in Panama, relocated to Ft. Bragg in August leaving only its Co. C at Ft. Davis, though the unit is still tasked with Latin American missions.

'Delta Force's' missions were sensitive and little has been revealed. Elements were known to have hit locations suspected of harboring Noriega, and were later present with the force surrounding the Papal Nunciatura. 'Delta Force' also stormed the Modelo Prison near *La Comandancía* with the aid of special ops. helicopters, losing an AH-6, and liberated the prisoners, including a US citizen held on espionage charges.

Navy SEALs executed several operations. Some elements secured the Canal's Pacific entrance, conducted rubber raiding boat patrols on the sea approaches to Howard AFB, and scuttled some PDF boats. TF White, composed of three SEAL Team 4 platoons, departed Howard AFB by helicopter well before H-Hour. They had deployed from US Naval Amphibious Base, Norfolk, Va., the day before, shortly after returning from a gruelling exercise in Florida. The force had launched their Zodiac raiding boats from the helicopters and assembled two miles off shore when they were notified that H-Hour had been advanced. They ran into shore, landed, and established security on one side of the Punta Paitilla Airport; their mission was to disable any aircraft that Noriega might escape in. Bravo Platoon began to block the runway by pushing light planes on to it as Golf Platoon approached the hangar housing Noriega's Lear Jet. The PDF opened fire on the platoon at close range, chewing up the lead squad. Bravo Platoon rushed to their aid and also took casualties. The SEALs directed heavy fire into the hangar and the

7th Inf. Div. Kawasaki KXT205-cc dirt bikes and Kawasaki four-wheel all-terrain vehicles are off-loaded at Howard AFB.

These specialized non-standard vehicles, painted matt black, are used by some scout platoons on an experimental basis. (DoD)

surviving PDF withdrew. The airport was secured, but four SEALs were dead and eight wounded. D/4-325 Abn. Inf. later reinforced the SEALs, and both units were relieved by A/2/75 Rangers.

Task Force Semper Fidelis

TF Semper Fi comprised a small HQ, MarFor, Panama; Marine Corps Security Force Co.; Co. K (+), 3d Bn., 6th Marines[1]; Co. D, 2d Lt. Armd. Inf. Bn. (LAI) reinforced by a provisional Scout Plt[1]; 1st Fleet Antiterrorist Security Team (FAST) Plt. (FAST Co., Marine Security Force Bn., Atlantic); and Det. G, Bde. Service Spt. Grp. 6. The Army's 534th MP Co. (16th MP Bde.) was attached to the TF. With the exception of the Security Force Co. at Rodman Naval Station, these units had been deployed as part of 'Nimrod Dancer' and had methodically rehearsed and refined their operation plan.

Their many and diversified missions began at 0100 hours, 20 Dec., with most elements operating in an area east of the Canal's Pacific entrance. The Security Co., K/3/6 Marines, and 534th MP Co. secured Rodman Naval Station, Naval Ammunition Depot, Howard AFB, and Arraijan Tank Farm. They also established roadblocks on the Inter-American Highway and secured several PDF installations in their area. The MPs operated a prisoner collection point, processing over 1,000, and conducted mounted security patrols. D/2 LAI Bn. and the FAST Plt. secured DNTT Station No. 2 and other small installations. The next day they took the 10th Military Zone HQ at La Chorrera 25 km west of the Canal. One D/2 LAI Bn. platoon was attached to TF Gator to take *La Comandancía* and was released back to the company in mid-January. On 28 Dec. the task force was augmented by Co. I (+), 3d Bn., 6th Marines[1]. TF Semper

---

[1] These units were provided by the 2d Marine Div., Camp Lejeune, NC.

Noriega's Lear Jet at Punta Paitilla Airport after being disabled by the SEALs of Task Force White. The damage appears to have been caused by LAWs, 40 mm grenades, and small arms. (Maj. B. A. Kilgariff)

Fi's follow-on missions included security tasks and conducting patrols through the area, more to promote goodwill than actual combat operations. D/2 LAI Bn. lost one dead and three Marines were wounded.

MP Operations

Military police units played a key rôle in 'Just Cause'. They were of particular value due to the initial security and prisoner/detainee collection operations, rear area security, and traffic circulation and control. Several of the units were engaged in direct combat while securing various PDF installations. The 401st MP Co. (89th MP Bde.) from Ft. Hood lost a man. Later they performed law enforcement functions, provided base security, policed dislocated persons compounds, and trained the new Panama Public Force.

MP units had begun rotating through Panama on four-month tours during 'Nimrod Dancer' in May 1989. They served alongside the in-country 92d MP Bn. (Provisional) and were under the control of the MP Command, US Army, South. The 519th MP Bn. had arrived just days earlier from Ft. George G. Meade, Md., to begin a 'Nimrod Sustain' rotation. XVIII Abn. Corps' 16th MP Bde. (Abn) deployed from Ft. Bragg shortly after D-Day along with its 503d MP Battalion. Almost a dozen MP companies attached to these battalions served in Panama, deploying from Forts Benning, Ga.; Bragg, NC; Meade, Md.; Hood, Tex.; Drum, NY; Lewis, Wash.; and Lee, Va. (MP

TF Aviation

The deployment of the Avn. Bde., 7th Inf. Div. began two days prior to D-Day when a command post was established at Howard AFB and took over control of TF Hawk, a group of aviation units supporting Operation 'Nimrod Dancer'. Designated TF Aviation, the force consisted of 1st Bn., 288th Avn. Regt. (assigned to US Army, South), elements of the 7th's and 82d's Divs. Avn. Bdes., and XVIII Abn. Corps' 18th Avn. Bde. (Airborne). The force was critically short of night vision goggle qualified crews, and some crews were supplied by other units in the States. There was also a shortage of door gunners, and ground support personnel were drafted and quickly trained. TF Hawk was formed from one company each of 1-288 Avn. and the 7th Inf. Div.'s 1st (Attack) and 2d (Assault) Bns., 123d Avn. to provide AH-1Ss and UH-60As for use in the Panama City area. Other 1-288 elements (TF 1-288) provided helicopter support to TF Atlantic. Team Wolf comprised AH-6 and AH-64 attack helicopters to support the Rangers at Rio Hato; the AH-64s were from the 82d Abn. Div.'s 1st Bn., 82d Aviation. The first AH-64 Apaches and their accompanying OH-58Cs had been flown into Howard AFB aboard C-5s in November and concealed in Hangar 1; more arrived later, to total eleven. Twenty special ops. AH/MH-6s were also airlifted in and concealed in hangars along with USAF MH-53J and MH-60D helicopters. These were flown during rehearsals only at night. The vast majority of initial flight operations were flown at night with the aid of night vision goggles. TF Condor was formed on 25 Dec. to support 2d Bde., 7th Inf. Division.

All in all, TF Aviation flew 5,000 hours during 'Just Cause',

Captured PDF weapons and vehicles at Albrook AFB. Beside the limousine are Chinese 75 mm Type 52 recoilless rifles, while behind it are four ZPU-4 anti-aircraft machine guns. (Capt. D. Hoagey)

about a third of these at night, performing air assault, fire support, troop and supplies lift, command and control, medical evacuation, and reconnaissance missions. Most fire support was in the form of machine guns and 20 mm and 30 mm cannons; only seven Hellfire missiles and some 2.75 in. rockets were fired, principally at *La Comandancía* and armored vehicles. The 160th Avn. Regt. lost two AH-6s (one to a wire strike) and one MH-6, while B/1-123 Avn. lost an OH-58C, resulting in an aviator being killed along with two from the 160th. Of the 167 helicopters committed, 41 were hit (exluding the four destroyed), but all were returned to action within 24 hours with the exception of a hard-landing shot-up UH-60A. Most of those that were hit were special ops. helicopters flying the most exposed missions.

SUMMARY & AFTERMATH

While one pessimistic defense analyst had predicted up to 1,000 US troops killed if Panama was invaded, the Joint Chiefs of Staff warned of a more realistic 70 dead. In all, 23 US servicemen (18 Army, four USN, one USMC) lost their lives, 330 were wounded, and two US female dependents died from PDF fire. The body of another US citizen was later discovered in one of the mass graves used to bury pre-'Just Cause' PDF victims. Most of the wounded were flown to Brooke Army Medical Center, Ft. Sam Houston, and Wilford Hall Medical Center, Lackland AFB, Tex., for treatment. There is speculation that a large percentage of the casualties were caused by friendly fire—one report suggests nine of the dead and 60 per cent of the wounded. This is probably exaggerated, but no doubt there were a number of friendly fire casualties. Except for a very small number of Vietnam and Grenada veterans, the troops, though well trained, had never experienced the confusion of night combat in urban areas.

The problem was compounded by the fact that most of the PDF wore uniforms almost identical to the US battle dress uniform, the same web gear, and in many cases the same helmets and weapons. Individual identification at night became a critical issue. This problem eased somewhat when most of the PDF began exchanging their uniforms for civilian clothes. (Some had simply discarded them in order to avoid capture, and were seen walking about in their underwear!) This caused another problem, however, making it almost impossible to differentiate PDF and Dig Bats from the civilian population.

Regrettably, this led to a number of civilian casualties due either to misidentification or simply to their being caught in a crossfire. For this reason an accurate determination of PDF and civilian casualties was impossible. Official American figures for PDF casualties listed 814 dead, several hundred wounded, and 4,054 detained. The unknown number of wounded is due to the fact that Panamanians in civilian clothes treated in hospitals and by the US military were counted as civilians, and the issue was not pressed at the time. The Army reported 220 Panamanian civilians killed, mostly in the vicinity of *La Comandancia*. Others died as a result of stray fire, mistaken identity, and foolishly attempting to run roadblocks (an 1800 to 0600 hours curfew was in effect). Accusations have been made that many more were killed and that the Army had attempted to conceal this by secret mass burials. Investigations have proven this to be unfounded, and the mass graves discovered after 'Just Cause' were filled with victims of Noriega's 'Boots'. An even larger number were killed by PDF and Dig Bat random sniping, revenge, arson, looting and robbery incidents. With thousands of weapons in circulation, the Army began a 'weapons for cash' program on 21 Dec., offering $150 for each turned in. An interagency document exploitation team was already at work sifting through thousands of PDF and government documents.

Noriega was narrowly missed by pursuing 'Delta Force' and SF troops on several occasions. At one point the Army had been given tips locating him in three different countries, 12 locations in Panama, and ten in Panama City. He commanded nothing and was aided only by a small group of henchmen whom he was still able to pay. Panamanian Radio did manage to broadcast taped messages urging resistance, but this was soon stopped. Noriega was discovered in the Papal Nunciatura, the equivalent to an embassy representing the Vatican. The area was blocked off and negotiations began for Noriega's surrender. Panamanian authorities wished him to be removed to the US and prosecuted, thus removing a rallying point for his supporters. Noriega sought political asylum from Cuba and Spain without success. The 4th

OA-37B Dragonfly aircraft of the USAF 24th Tactical Spt. Sdn. prepares to launch on a mission sortie from Howard AFB. Its camouflage colors are dark gray and forest green with the tail marking 'HW'. (24th Composite Wing)

An M16A1-armed member of the USAF's 24th Security Police Sdn. guarding the main gate at Howard AFB. (DoD)

Psyops. Gp. played loud rock music in an effort to un-nerve Noriega. The musical score included such selections as *Voodoo Child, You're No Good; Nowhere to Run, Nowhere to Hide*; and *I Fought the Law and the Law Won*.

Following much negotiation, and some 20,000 Panamanians marching on the Papal Nunciatura to demand that he give up, Noriega surrendered to Gen. Maxwell Thurman on 3 January. He was rushed to a Night Hawk helicopter and flown to Howard AFB, where he was formally arrested by DEA officials, placed aboard an MC-130, and flown to Florida for arraignment by federal court—all in just over 30 minutes. This was followed by the arrest of several of Noriega's key officers, though others managed to elude apprehension. The new government charged almost 900 former PDF officers with crimes ranging from abuse of power to corruption.

Throughout Operation 'Just Cause' the vast majority of the Panamanian people were totally supportive of the US action. Countless examples of Panamanians supporting US soldiers were recorded, including aiding wounded, hiding separated soldiers from the PDF, pointing out PDF positions and movements, giving the locations of weapon caches, and providing food and drink. Some commanders remarked on the difficulties they had in keeping an eye on the troops as young ladies offered other favors.

Operation 'Just Cause' was terminated on 31 Jan. 1990. Now, the difficult task of rebuilding the shattered country and aiding a struggling embryo government lay ahead.

Operation 'Promote Liberty'

Teams from various US government agencies began arriving in-country within days of D-Day. Surveys were undertaken and efforts began to restore law and order as well as public services. The most pressing need was to house several thousand dislocated persons. Scores of Army Reserve civil affairs personnel, volunteering for the duty, began arriving as part of the Civil Military Operations TF formed on 22 December. These men and women were invaluable to the new government because of their civilian skills ranging from police supervisors and public utilities specialists to councilmen from major metropolitan cities.

It was obviously vital to re-establish law and order. The Panama Public Force (*Fuerza Publica de Panamá*—FPP) was quickly formed and training began under US guidance. Unfortunately former FP personnel were the only trained personnel available; this understandably led to mistrust among the population, until they demonstrated otherwise, and this still exists to some degree. The exiled Col. Eduardo Hassan returned to Panama and was placed in command of the FPP; he was later forced to resign.

Several 7th Inf. Div. and 193d Inf. Bde. units continued search and clear operations within Panama City, other urban areas, and the countryside looking for renegade PDF and Dig Bat personnel. On 21 Feb. eleven 7th Inf. Div. and 1-228th Avn. personnel were killed in two separate weather-caused helicopter crashes while conducting these operations. As late as March 1990 16 US service men and 11 Panamanians were wounded in a grenade attack by Noriega loyalists.

The US has funnelled millions of dollars into Panama in an attempt to boost the shattered economy, and has provided extensive civil-military assistance. Panamanian agencies are attempting to recover hidden funds and property stolen by Noriega's mafia. The country faces a long, hard road to economic recovery and political stability. The first Panamanian admini-

strator of the bi-national Panama Canal Commission was sworn in during Sept. 1990. The US still plans to turn over the Canal in the year 2000.

Noriega's thirst for power went far beyond Panama's borders. From about 1985 until 1989 Col. Mohamed Ali Seineldin, a forcibly retired Argentinian Army officer of Arab extraction, worked for Noriega as a senior instructor at Panama's Military Institute. Noriega arranged for his secret return to Argentina and financed his plan to overthrow the legal government. Though Seineldin was arrested in Oct. 1990, Argentine army troops hailing him as their 'legitimate' leader staged yet another unsuccessful coup attempt on 3 Dec. 1990.

In mid-Dec. 1990, almost a year after 'Just Cause', the former FPP commander Eduardo Hassan led an ineffectual rebellion by about 100 of the 12,000-man FPP; US 193d Inf. Bde. troops put down the revolt, killing one rebel. US troops were used rather than forcing other FPP to take up arms against their comrades.

Capt. Asunción Gaitan, a Noriega aide and head of a secret intelligence operation, had sought refuge in the Papal Nunciatura with his mentor; remaining there after Noriega's surrender, he disappeared on 16 Sept. 1990. With a reputation as a ruthless hothead, he is also cunning and intelligent. Completely loyal to Noriega, he has reputedly laid plans to organize a subversive movement within Panama.

The tasks given Joint Task Force South by President Bush had been accomplished. Though some aspects of Operation 'Just Cause' were controversial, as any military action will be, the end result is what counts. Another third-rate tyrant was disposed of, a funnel for drug traffic was closed, and a repressed nation's self-determination was returned to the people. Their difficulties are not yet over, but at least they are on the road to recovery. The US armed forces learned much in the way of command and control, deployment logistics, and tactical training needs. These lessons were to serve the military well: within months US forces began deploying to Saudi Arabia in support of Operation 'Desert Shield', planned and co-ordinated by some of the same staffs responsible for 'Just Cause'.

THE PLATES

A: Stand in the Door! Inbound to Rio Hato Drop Zone, 0002 hours, 20 December
Troops of the 2d Bn., 75th Ranger Regt. await the last jump command, 'Go!', as their C-130H hurtles toward Rio Hato Military Base and H-Hour.
A1: Ranger
The Rangers wear Kevlar® helmets, lightweight Battle Dress Uniforms (BDU), and tropical combat boots, usually referred to as jungle boots. Their parachutes are standard static line-deployed, non-steerable T-10s. Slung under the reserve parachutes are All-Purpose Lightweight Individual Carrying Equipment (ALICE) large combat packs, more commonly called rucksacks, or simply 'rucks'. ALICE web gear was worn under the parachute harness. Individual weapons were carried in M1951 weapons containers.
A2: Ranger Jumpmaster
The jumpmaster conducts pre-jump refresher training, inspects each jumper after his equipment is donned, ensures all safety requirements are met, gives the jump commands, and will follow his stick out the door.

The sign says it all: Panama City, Christmas Day 1989. (Maj. B. A. Kilgariff)

A3: USAF Loadmaster

The loadmaster aids the jumpmaster and relays information between the jumpmaster and pilot. He wears a ripcord-activated 5OC7024 parachute, a standard aircrew emergency rig (see Plate L3 for other uniform items). The 75th Ranger Regt. scroll is shown inset; the battalions have 1st, 2nd, or 3rd on the left end of the tab and Bn. on the right.

B: The 'Maximum Leader'

Like many past dictators, Brig. Gen. Manuel Antonio Noriega had an affection for unique uniforms. One observer reported he had a different pattern camouflage uniform and cap for every occasion. (These camouflage patterns were not worn by other PDF personnel.) Besides Panamanian, his jumpwings included Israeli and Peruvian.

B1: Noriega wearing a 'duck hunter' camouflage uniform modelled after standard jungle fatigues. The leather belt is worn only by PDF generals.

B2: Noriega in a splinter pattern camouflage uniform.

B3: Noriega outfitted in a formal service uniform.

B4: Noriega in a 'tiger stripe' camouflage uniform with subdued insignia embroidered directly on to it.

B5: Noriega wearing the PDF officer's service uniform. The PDF patch was worn on the left shoulder of most uniforms (inset).

C: Noriega's 'Boots'

Besides regular PDF troops, Noriega employed several other organizations to exploit his citizens and ensure his regime's survival.

C1: Panamanian Police Force officer

Uniformed and equipped as typical municipal police, many of the FP preyed on the citizens they were sworn to protect. Principally armed with .38 Special S & W M-10-2 revolvers and night-sticks, the police also possessed assault rifles and shotguns. Only small numbers of the FP actively opposed the US intervention. The standard FP patch is inset; others existed.

C2: Police Force 2d Anti-riot Co. officer

Members of the 2d Anti-riot Co. '*Centurion*' were selected from among FP officers of proven loyalty. They were armed with M16A1 rifles, Federal Laboratories 38 mm tear gas guns, and Federal Laboratories Model 515 triple chaser tear gas hand grenades (which separate into three sections on impact). This second-corporal is outfitted with US ALICE web gear and a US M17 gas mask. Subdued black on olive green patches and chevrons were also worn.

C3: Special Security Anti-terrorist Unit soldier

Like the 1st Anti-riot Co. FP officers, UESAT personnel were selected from soldiers of demonstrated loyalty, since they were also employed as Noriega's bodyguards. Besides this 9 mm Uzi sub-machine gun the small force was armed with sniper rifles, RPG-7 rocket launchers, and other weapons. They were also equipped with body armor and weapon night sights. Besides this WAT-type uniform and gear, the UESAT also used PDF camouflage uniforms and a black beret (on which the inset badge was worn).

C4: Dignity Battalion member

During parades and when out playing goon squad it was usual for the Dig Bats to wear red T-shirts proclaiming their identity. This particular pattern T-shirt was worn by the unit which beat up opposition leaders in the streets during the May elections. Another version had black lettering. Some members simply wore plain red T-shirts, and other units used black-trimmed blue T-shirts. This 'uniform' was completed by blue jeans or other dark slacks and various colour tennis shoes. She is armed with an M2 carbine.

D1: Mortarman, 1st Bde., 82d Abn. Division

Like most troops committed to 'Just Cause' this mortar gunner is wearing both components of the Personal Armor System for Ground Troops (PASGT), the helmet, ground troops, and a Kevlar® 9-lb. body armor, fragmentation protective vest, ground troops. The 60 mm M224 lightweight mortar began to replace the 81 mm M29A1 at company level in the mid-1980s. Greatly improved over the earlier 60 mm M19, used by Ranger companies until replaced by the M224, it has almost the same range and only slightly less lethality than the 81 mm. While it is normally equipped with a conventional M7 base plate and bipod, this one is fitted with an M8 base plate for use in the hand-held mode. His personal armament is a 9mm M9 pistol in an ambidextrous M12 holster. The 'All American Division's' patch is inset.

D2: Grenadier, 5-87th Inf., 193d Inf. Brigade

All US troops wore a US flag sewn or safety-pinned to their right shoulder and a stripe of white tape tied around their left upper arm as identification. This M203 grenade launcher-armed grenadier carries up to 20 HE and four longer pyrotechnic 40 mm rounds in a grenade carrier vest. Most troops carried M17A2 protective masks in case CS (tear gas) was employed. The Brigade's patch is inset.

D3: Radio/Telephone Operator, 4-6th Inf., 5th Inf. Division

Heavy mechanized infantrymen tend to travel lighter than their heavily burdened light infantry counterparts—somewhat of a contradiction—this rifle platoon RTO carries an AN/PRC-77

Safe conduct pass printed by the 1st Psyops. Bn. and distributed by US Army, South. These were printed on reverse sides of the same slip. (SSgt. M. Brocksmith, USAF)

radio providing a link to the company command group and the other platoons. A few units were outfitted with the older body armor, fragmentation protective vest with $\frac{3}{4}$ collar, M69. Helmet camouflage bands are issued with two tabs of fluorescent tape sewn on; these 'ranger eyes' permit a following man to retain visual contact in total darkness. The 'Red Diamond Division's' patch is inset.

E1: SAW Gunner, 2d Bde., 7th Inf. Division

The 2d Bde. deployed to Panama outfitted in standard (heavy-weight) BDUs, leather combat boots, and cold weather clothing in the belief that they were flying to Ft. Bragg for an exercise—all part of the deception plan. Later deploying units wore light-weight BDUs and jungle boots. The helmet's tangle of camouflage strips (made from burlap, BDU fabric, and/or plastic camouflage net garnishing), called 'ragtops' or 'cabbage patch hats', is a virtual trademark of the 7th Inf. Division. This squad automatic weapon (SAW) gunner is armed with the M249E1; a 200-round belt is carried in the plastic magazine in the large belt pouch and standard 30-round M16 magazines in the smaller ALICE pouch—these also fit in the SAW. All light infantry units carry the large ALICE rucksack. The 'Bayonet Division's' patch is inset. In the background is a Kawasaki four-wheel all-terrain vehicle used by scouts.

SAFE CONDUCT PASS

THIS PASS IS FOR USE BY PDF, DIGNITY BATTALION, AND CODEPADI MEMBERS. THE BEARER OF THIS PASS, UPON PRESENTING IT TO ANY U.S. MILITARY MEMBER, WILL BE GUARANTEED SAFE PASSAGE TO U.S. FACILITIES THAT WILL PROVIDE MEDICAL ATTENTION, FOOD, AND SHELTER.

[signature]

GENERAL MARC A. CISNEROS
CG, US ARMY SOUTH

SAFE CONDUCT PASS

PASAPORTE A LA LIBERTAD

ESTE PASAPORTE ES PARA EL USO DE MIEMBROS DE LA F.F.D.D., BATALLON DE LA DIGNIDAD Y LA CODEPADI. SI SE PRESENTA ESTE BOLETO DE LOS ESTADOS UNIDOS, LE GARANTIZAMOS SU SEGURIDAD, ACCESO A FACILIDADES MEDICAS, COMIDA, Y UN LUGAR DE DESCANSO Y RECUPERACION. RECUERDEN; NO HAY QUE SUFRIR MAS.

[signature]

GENERAL MARC A. CISNEROS
COMANDANTE DE TROPAS DEL EJERCITO SUR

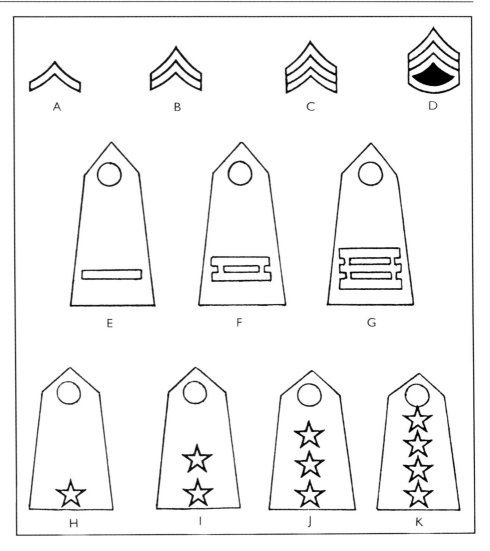

PDF Rank Insignia. Soldier (Soldado) had no insignia. (A) 2nd Corporal/Cabo 2°. (B) 1st Corporal/Cabo 1°. (C) 2nd Sergeant/Sargento 2°. (D) 1st Sergeant/Sargento 1°. Enlisted full-color rank insignia were gold yellow on dark green (as US Army), black on olive green (subdued), and small gold-colored metal pin-on for headgear. (E) Sub-Lieutenant/Subteniente. (F) Lieutenant/Teniente. (G) Captain/Capitán. (H) Major/Mayor. (I) Lieutenant Colonel/Teniente Coronel. (J) Colonel/Coronel. (K) Brigadier General/General de Brigada. Officers' rank insignia were gold-colored metal (service and dress uniforms), gold yellow on olive green cloth tab (garrison uniforms), and black on olive green cloth tab or black metal pin-on (field uniforms). (USMC)

E2: Sniper, 1st Bde., 7th Inf. Division.

'Light Fighters' place a great deal of emphasis on sniping, as they do on all other combat and fieldcraft skills. While the M21 sniper rifle, based on the M14, is still in wide use, the new 7.62 mm M24 sniper system is being issued. Based on the Remington Model 700 bolt-action rifle, it mounts a 9× scope. Snipers were employed to provide US roadblocks with protective fire and as countersnipers. A 1 × 2-inch strip of GLINT tape was fixed to all troops' helmet tops; this can be detected by a Gated Laser Illuminator for Night Television, a night vision system mounted on AC-130 gunships and some other special ops. aircraft, enabling friendly troops to be identified even from several thousand feet up. The no longer standard issue M1956 (canvas) or M1961 (nylon) combat or 'butt' pack is carried by many 'Light Fighters'.

E3: Tactical Air Control Party member, Det. 5, 602d Tactical Air Control Wing, 7th Inf. Division

USAF TACPs co-ordinated close air support for their battalions via man-packed AN/PRC-113 UHF/VHF radios and other specialized radios mounted in HMMWVs. Most TACP person-nel were armed with GAU-5 carbines (USAF shortened version of M16A2) and M9 pistols in M11 shoulder holsters (intended for the .45-cal. M1911A1). Equipment includes an old M1956 magazine pouch, SDU-5/E strobe light, and K-bar knife. USAF personnel wear the same uniform as the Army unit they are attached to, but with USAF rank, unit patches, and other unique insignia. The 602d TACW patch (also inset) is on the left pocket, Tactical Air Command patch on the right, and the Combat Crew Badge over it. Most personnel wore the Army unit's patch on the left shoulder as well, while others wore the flyers' suit style black leather name tag rather than the cloth name and USAF tapes.

E4: Air Liaison Officer, Det. 5, 602d Tactical Air Control Wing, 7th Inf. Division

USAF TACP personnel wear a black beret with a common flash when not in the field. TACP air liaison officers wore the same USAF unit patches as enlisted men, but with the addition of a 27th Tactical Air Spt. Sdn. patch over the right pocket, and seldom wore the Combat Crew Badge. Unlike the Army's two-tone subdued patches, the USAF uses muted shades of the full color versions; (called 'vivid' by the USAF).

A — BATALLON PAZ · FUERZAS DE DEFENSA

B — 4º BATALLON CEMACO · LA SELVA ES NUESTRA ALIADA

C — BATALLON 2000

D — TIGRES · TINAJITA

E — 2ª COMPAÑIA INF. · PUMAS

F — DIABLO ROJO

G — 4TA COMPAÑIA INF. · URRACA

H — LOS CHOLOS · VICTORIANO · 5TA CIA · INF · LORENZO

I — 6TA COMPAÑIA INF. · MEC. · EXPEDICIONARIA

J — MACHO DE MONTE

K — POLICIA · 8VA CIA · INF · MILITAR

L — ESCUADRON DE CABALLERIA · LEALTAD SIN PRECIO NI DUDA · DRAGONES · AL COMANDANTE EN JEFE · JOSE ANTONIO REMON CANTERA

M — FUERZA AEREA PANAMEÑA · HALCON GRIS · DESDE EL AIRE LEALTAD · FUERZAS DE DEFENSA

N — MARINA · PANAMA

O — FUERZA DE POLICIA · FUERZAS DE DEFENSA

F1: 'Delta Force' Assault Team operator
Available information on this unit is rather sparse, but members are permitted a certain amount of latitude in the selection of uniforms and equipment. Apparently, many wore CWU-27/P flyer's coveralls during their initial direct action missions, and few wore headgear; others wore standard BDUs or black SWAT-type suits. The only insignia worn was the US flag. A wide variety of privately purchased boots were used, in this case Hi Techs, along with mixes of the Individual Tactical Load Bearing Vest (ITLBV) and ALICE components over a PASGT body armor vest. The ITLBV, a component of the Integrated Individual Fighting System, was to have been issued in 1988, but was delayed due to development problems. The sound-suppressed sub-machine gun is a 9 mm H & K MP5A3S, and he is equipped with the new, extremely lightweight AN/PVS-7A night vision goggles with special head-mounted imaging assembly. The US Army Special Operations Command patch is inset.

F2: Special Forces trooper, A/3/7th SFGA
SF troopers tended to wear BDUs without any insignia other than the US flag. Headgear varied, in this case a tropical hat, more commonly known as the 'boonie hat'. SF generally uses standard weapons, here an M16A2 and 84 mm M136 LAW, as used to engage PDF armored vehicles at the Pacora River Bridge. The Special Forces patch is inset.

F3: Navy SEAL Team 4 member
The SEALs wore common uniforms, but were permitted much leeway in equipment selection. Lightweight BDUs were worn with jungle boots and ALICE gear. While boonie hats were common, other forms of headgear sometimes provided a piratical appearance. He wears a dive watch, wrist compass, and laser-safe goggles. Nomex® and leather GS/FRP-2 flyer's gloves complete his outfit. A variety of weapons are employed, including this M16A1 carbine fitted with a Beta C-MAG 100-round twin drum. Other weapons include M16A1 rifles, M203 grenade-launchers, M60 machine guns, MP5A3 sub-machine guns, and LAWs. When operating in close proximity to water they wear various model flotation vests under their jackets. The Naval Special Warfare Badge is inset.

G1: Military Policeman, 401st MP Co., 89th MP Brigade
MPs are armed with both an M16A2 rifle and M9 pistol. ALICE web gear and other combat equipment was standard, and typical MP garrison trappings (semi-glossy black insignia-adorned helmet liner and police-style black leather gear) are not worn in combat. The Naugahyde (artificial leather) brassard usually bore the MP unit's parent formation's shoulder patch. Most units deploying to Panama replaced this with a US flag. In some cases a white tape stripe was tied over the US flag as an additional indentification.

G2: Military Policeman, 108th MP Co., 16th MP Bde. (Airborne)
Some MP units deploying to Panama after 'Just Cause' began retained the unit patch on their brassard, in this case a subdued version; a few units wore the brassard on the right arm. Some personnel also attached additional US flags to their helmets to aid identification. The Brigade's patch is inset.

G3: MP Humvee
Each three-man MP team is transported by an M1025 High Mobility Multipurpose Wheeled Vehicle (HMMWV) armament carrier mounting an M60 machine gun. One-inch squares of GLINT tape were fixed to the four top corners of many vehicles. Six HMMWV-mounted MP teams comprise a platoon, three platoons a company.

G4: Light truck driver, A/193d Forward Spt. Battalion
Numerous combat service support personnel became actively engaged in combat—there were no front lines in Panama. Though female soldiers are prohibited from combat assignments, they will be found in headquarters and support units down to combined arms brigade level, and many combat support assignments potentially place women in position to be engaged in direct combat. All support personnel are expected to be proficient to defend themselves and their installations, regardless of sex. Many of these units are still armed with the older M16A1 rifle. There is no difference between male and female field uniforms.

H1: LAV-25 Light Armored Vehicle, D/2d LAI Battalion
A LAV-25 is crewed by a vehicle commander, gunner, driver, and four infantry scouts. The 17-ton LAV-25's armament is a 25 mm M242 Bushmaster chain gun, 7.62 mm coaxial M240C and pintle-mounted M240E1 machine guns, and eight smoke grenade dischargers.

H2: LAV-25 vehicle commander, D/2d LAI Battalion
Other than the DH132 Combat Vehicle Crewman's (CVC) helmet, LAV crewmen wear the same uniforms as other Marines.

H3: 1st Fleet Antiterrorist Security Team Plt. member
Attached to D/2d LAI Bn., the 1st FAST Plt. cleared PDF installations using its close-quarter battle skills, to which it devotes a great deal of training time and ammunition. Platoon members wore reversed utility caps rather than helmets to ensure maximum vision and hearing inside buildings. A strip of GLINT tape was fixed to the 'cover's' top crown. FAST Plt. weapons include stun grenades, M16A2 rifles, M203 grenade launchers, M249E1 SAWs, 12 ga. Mossberg Model 590 riot shotguns (inset), and 9 mm Colt M16 sub-machine guns, as carried by this Marine. He has a SWAT-type magazine carrier and M1961 'butt' pack. Flashlights were sometimes attached to weapons or gloves by Velcro® for use when searching dark rooms.

H4: SMAW Gunner, K/3/6th Marines
The 83 mm MK 153 MOD 0 Shoulder-launched Multi-purpose Assault Weapon, mounting an integral 9 mm MK 8 MOD 0 spotting rifle, is a building- and bunker-buster rather than an anti-armor weapon. The gunner is armed with an M9 pistol and M9 multi-purpose wire-cutter bayonet. Like all Marines, he carries a small first aid kit on his belt.

PDF Shoulder Patches. Full-color unit patches were worn on the right shoulder of all uniforms. Units authorized berets (indicated by including the beret color) wore their patch on it, over the left temple. Subdued patches were worn on olive green field uniforms, but seldom on camouflage. Most are 2½ inches in diameter. The PDF patch (see Plate B5) was worn on the left shoulder of all uniforms. (A) 2d Bn. 'Paz'. (B) 4th Bn. 'Cemaco'. (C) Bn. 2000—maroon beret. (D) 1st Inf. Combat and Fire Spt. Co. 'Tigre'. (E) 2d Inf. Abn. Co. 'Puma'—maroon beret. (F) 3d Inf. Co. 'Diablo Rojo'–maroon beret. (G) 4th Inf. Co. 'Urraca'— subdued on lime green beret—disbanded in Oct. 1989. (H) 5th Inf. Co., MP Bn. (I) 6th Inf. Mech. Expeditionary Co. (J) 7th Inf. Co. 'Macho de Monte'—black beret. (K) 8th Inf. Co., MP Bn. (L) Cav. Sdn. 'Gen. Jose Antonio Ramon Cantera'. (M) Air Force. (N) National Naval Force. (O) Police Force. All other PDF organizations also possessed patches or tabs.

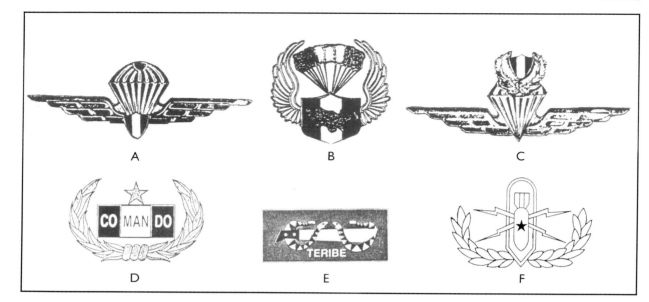

A   B   C

D   E   F

PDF Skill Badges. Metal full-color badges were normally worn on the left chest and sometimes on the beret or field cap. Full-color and black subdued embroidered versions also exist. All shields were blue-white-red from viewer's left to right. (A) Parachutist—gold wings and canopy. (B) Freefall Parachutist—gold wings, blue-white-red canopy, green jumper, black boots. (C) Instructor Parachutist—gold wings, canopy, wreath. (D) Commando—gold wreath, star and COMANDO, blue-white-red bar. (E) Jungle Survival—dark pink backing, blue and orange snakes, white and black bolo. (F) Explosive, Demolition and Sabotage—gold with black star.

I: PDF uniforms

The PDF wore uniforms almost identical to US BDUs. They were outfitted with both US jungle boots and ALICE web gear; the 'U.S.' printed on the gear was obscured by black paint, often with 'FFDD' overprinted in green. M16 ammunition pouches were replaced by East German 'dashed print' camouflage pouches for personnel armed with AKs. Besides the camouflage uniform, olive green garrison uniforms with either full-color or subdued insignia were used. A wide variety of headgear was worn.

I1: 1st Inf. Combat and Fire Spt. Co. 'Tigre'

This unit had three rifle platoons plus an anti-tank and two mortar sections. This gunner is manning a US 90mm M67 recoilless rifle. Like all units organic or attached to Bn. 2000, it was outfitted with US Kevlar® helmets. Its patch is inset.

I2: 2d Inf. Abn. Co. 'Puma'

Composed of an interior guard and three rifle platoons, mortar section, and Dets. 'Chepo' and 'Cañitas', it was parachute qualified. Many *paracaidistas* wore their jumpwings on their beret beside the unit patch (also inset). This *teniente* also wears his rank and the Jungle Survival School badge beneath his wings. He wears jungle fatigues with embroidered 'RP' and infantry crossed rifles devices.

I3: 3d Inf. Co. 'Diablo Rojo'

This unit was composed of three rifle platoons, a special unit (with light armed vehicles), and mortar and interior guard sections. Besides a maroon beret, it also used this jungle hat. He is armed with a camouflaged Soviet RPG-7 rocket launcher. The unit patch is inset.

I4: 5th Inf. Co., MP Bn. 'Victoriano Lorenzo'

This MP wears a parade service uniform and is armed with a Taiwanese 5.56mm T-65 rifle and Belgian 9mm FN-Browning Hi-Power pistol. The unit patch is inset.

I5: Co. A 'Fortuna', 2d Bn. 'Paz'

While this unit wore olive green uniforms in garrison, in the field they wore a mix of civilian clothes and military uniform. The field cap is standard PDF issue. He is armed with an Israeli Soltam 60mm mortar and Soviet AK-47 assault rifle. The unit patch is inset.

J1: PDF V-150 APC, 6th Mech. Inf. Company

The 6th Co.'s 13 Cadillac Gage 5-ton V-150 APCs were armed with .50-cal. M2 and 7.62mm M60 machine guns. The unit had a fire support platoon (V-300s), three infantry mechanized platoons (V-150s) plus anti-tank, mortar, and maintenance sections. Crewmen wore the US DH132 CVC helmet while dismountable troops wore the US Kelvar® helmet, often with goggles, or an 'Afrika Korps' style cap. Tan T-shirts and shorts were sometimes used in lieu of the camouflage uniform. The unit patch is inset.

J2: PDF V-300 Fire Support Vehicle, Bn. 2000

Mounting a Belgian Cockerill 90mm Mk III gun, the 10-ton V-300 equipped Bn. 2000's Mech. Company. It also mounted two 7.62mm machine guns; the turretless APC version had two pintle-mounted M60 machine guns. The battalion's patch is inset.

K: 'La Noche de Fuego' (The Night of Fire); Inside La Comandancia

Elements of several PDF units defended *La Comandancia* on 20 Dec. 1989.

K1: 6th Mech. Inf. Company
This first-corporal is armed with an East German 7.62 mm MPiKMS-72, an improved version of the Soviet AKMS. His full-color unit patch (Plate J1) is printed on his T-shirt's left chest.

K2: 7th Inf. Co. 'Macho de Monte'
Armed with a West German 40 mm H & K grenade pistol and T-65 rifle, this second-sergeant wears his unit patch on a camouflage beret. A Soviet RPG-18 rocket launcher rests against the wall along with Soviet RGD-5 grenades. The 7th Co. had an interior guard and three rifle platoons plus sections of Commandos, Frogmen, and Explosives, along with the motorcycle-equipped Motorized Section 'Cocuyos Montañeros'.

K3: Maneuver Co. 'Furia', Bn. 2000
This soldier wears the garrison uniform with full-color insignia and is armed with a Belgian 7.62 mm FN MAG machine gun.

L1: US Army UH-60A aviator, 1-288th Aviation
This chief warrant officer 2 wears the SPH-4 flight helmet, Nomex® fire-resistant olive green shade 106 CWU-27/P flyer's coveralls (used by all services), and GS/FRP-2 flyer's gloves. The individual's aviator wings, rank, and name are embossed on a Velcro® fastened leather nameplate. The steel-toed flyer's boots use 'D' rings rather than eyelets to prevent burns. The US Army, South patch is inset.

L2: USAF OA-37B pilot, 24th Tactical Spt. Squadron
The HGU-55/P flyer's helmet with MBU-12/P oxygen mask, CSU-13B/P cutaway anti-G suit, LPU-9/P 'horse collar' automatic life preserver (replacing the LPU-3/P underarm type), sage green CWU-27/P flyer's coveralls, GS/FRP-2 gloves, and parachute harness make up this captain's ensemble. Under all this is an SRU-21/P survival vest containing an S & W .38-cal. Special M13 revolver, survival knife, AN/PRC-90 radio, MK13 MOD 0 flares, medical kit, and other items. The silver cuff stars each indicate 500 flying hours; gold stars indicate like combat hours. The squadron's parent 24th Composite Wing patch is inset.

L3: USAF AC-130H Gunner, 16th Special Ops. Squadron
This staff sergeant wears the HGU-26/P helmet with an M87 intercom, sage green CWU-27/P flyer's coveralls, and GR/FRP-1 gloves. The snow shovel is an essential piece of equipment needed to clear the mountains of expended 20 mm cases and links. The squadron's patch is inset.

Notes sur les planches en couleur
Note: Veuillez comparer ces brèves descriptions avec les légendes des gravures en anglais pour obtenir des détails supplémentaires; nous n'avons pas répété ici les listes des désignations d'équipement qui étaient intraduisibles.

A Le 2nd Bataillon du 75ème Régiment de Rangers approche la zone de largage à Rio Hato. A1 C'est un soldat typique de cette unité, avec casque 'Fritz' Kevlar, uniforme de camouflage BDU de type léger tropical, bottes de jungle, et parachute T-10. Son sac à dos du dispositif ALICE est passé en bandoulière sur l'épaule au-dessous du parachute de réserve, les ceinturons et poches ALICE sont portés au-dessous du harnais de parachute, et les armes sont transportées dans des conteneurs M1951. A2 L'instructeur de saut des Rangers, sautera le dernier. A3 C'est le Chef de chargement de l'US Air Force; bien qu'il porte un parachute de secours il ne sautera pas avec les troupes. En cartouche, insigne d'épaule portant le numéro de bataillon des Rangers.

B Une variété d'uniformes préférés à des moments variés par le Général Noriega, nombreux sont ceux qui lui sont uniques. Il portait des 'ailes' panaméennes, israéliennes et péruviennes. B4 Uniforme de service officiel des FDP, avec insigne d'épaule de nationalité.

C1 Officier de la Police panaméenne, avec insigne d'épaule en cartouche. C2 Caporal subalterne de la 2nde Compagnie anti-émeutes de la Police, une unité d'élite lourdement armée. Comme de nombreuses troupes panaméennes, il a un équipement en toile de fabrication américaine. C3 Soldat de l'Unité de Sécurité Spéciale anti-terroriste, qui fournissait aussi les gardes du corps de Noriega. Lorsqu'ils portaient l'uniforme de camouflage, ils avaient un béret noir avec l'insigne en cartouche ici. C4 Les 'Bataillons de la Dignité' étaient des civils, armés mais sans uniforme, qui agissaient comme escadrons de gros bras pour Noriega. Très peu résistèrent contre l'invasion des Etats-Unis.

D1 Armure de corps et casque PASGT; et mortier léger de 60 mm M224, avec ici une plaque d'assise spéciale utilisée pour le tenir à la main. L'arme personnelle du soldat chargé du mortier est le pistolet M9. En cartouche, l'insigne de brigade. D2 Toutes les troupes US portaient l'écusson du drapeau national sur leur manche pour être identifiées rapidement, et un ruban blanc autour du bras gauche. Le gilet pour transporter les grenades de ce soldat qui est armé d'un M203 contient 20 explosifs et quatre grenades incendiaires plus longues. Des masques M17A2 portés au cas des gaz seraient utilisés. En cartouche, l'insigne de brigade. D3 Des radios AN/PRC-77 reliaient les pelotons et leur groupe de commandement des compagnies. Certaines unités portaient toujours le gilet blindé M69. Deux écussons fluorescents fixés sur la bande du casque se voyaient de nuit pour les hommes qui suivaient derrière. En cartouche, l'insigne de division.

E1 Cette brigade vint à Panama dans des uniformes de poids normal et des bottes de cuir; et est connue en particulier pour l'enchevêtrement du camouflage qu'elle portait sur son casque. La vaste poche sur le ceinturon contient un chargeur pour bande de 200 coups pour la mitraillette M249, les chargeurs pour fusil M16 à 30 coups sont transportés dans la poche plus petite et peuvent aussi être chargés sur cette arme. En cartouche, l'insigne de division. E2 Tireurs d'élite avec fusils M21 ou les nouveaux M24. Une bande de ruban réflecteur sur le sommet du casque peut être détectée par un dispositif de vision spécial de nuit qui transportaient plusieurs avions US, repérant les troupes amies même à haute altitude. Les anciens sacs de combat M56 ou M61 continuent à être utilisés par de nombreux soldats de l'infanterie légère. E3 Contrôleur au sol des Forces aériennes accompagnant les

Farbtafeln
Anmerkung: Vergleichen Sie diese kurzen Bemerkungen mit den englischsprachigen Bildtexten zu den Farbtafeln für genauere Details; wir haben hier eine Reihe unübersetzbarer Namen von Ausrüstungsgegenständen nicht wiedergegeben.

A Das 2. Bataillon des 75. Ranger-Regiments nähert sich dem Absprunggebiet von Rio Hato. A1 Ein typischer Soldat dieser Einheit, mit einem Kevlar-'Fritz'-Helm, BDU-Tarnuniform tropischer Art, Dschungelstiefeln und T-10-Fallschirm. Sein ALICE-Rucksack liegt unter dem Reservefallschirm, sein ALICE-Riemenzeug wird unter dem Gurtwerk des Fallschirms getragen, die Waffen in M1951-Behältern. A2 Der Ranger-Absprung-Ausbilder springt als letzter ab. A3 Der US Air Force Loadmaster; obwohl er einen Notfallschirm trägt, springt er nicht mit ab. Das numerierte Schulterabzeichen des Ranger-Bataillons ist gesondert zu sehen.

B Eine Vielfalt von Uniformen, die alle von General Noriega getragen wurden — viele davon ausschließlich von ihm. Er trug 'Schwingen' der Fallschirmjäger von Panama, Israel und Peru. B4 Offizielle Dienstuniform der FDP, mit nationalen Schulerabzeichen.

C1 Polizeioffizier aus Panama; siehe separate Schulterabzeichen. C2 Polizeikorporal der 2. Anti-Riot-Kompanie, einer schwer bewaffneten Elite-Einheit. Wie so viele panamanische Truppen trägt er in den USA hergestelltes Riemenzeug. C3 Soldat der UESAT, der speziellen Antiterroristeneinheit, die auch als Leibwache von General Noriega fungierte. Wenn in Tarnuniform, trugen sie eine schwarze Kappe mit Abzeichen (separat gezeigt). C4 Die sog. 'Dignity Battalions' waren bewaffnet, aber nicht uniformierte Zivilisten, die als politische Schergen Noriegas fungierten. Nur wenige von ihnen leisten der amerikanischen Invasion Widerstand.

D1 Kugelfeste PASGT-Kleidung und Helm; leichter 60 mm-Mörser M224, hier mit spezieller Fußplatte für handgehaltenen Abschuß. Persönliche Bewaffnung des Mörserschützen ist eine M9-Pistole. Siehe separat die Schulterabzeichen der 82. Division. D2 Alle US-Truppen trugen zur raschen Identifizierung das Flaggenabzeichen am Armel und ein weißes Band um den linken Arm. Die mit Granaten versehene Weste dieses Mannes, der mit einer M203 bewaffnet ist, enthält 20 Sprenggranaten und 4 längere Brandgranaten. Für den Fall von Gasangriffen wurde eine M17A2-Gasmaske getragen. Siehe separat das Brigadeabzeichen. D3 Die AN/PRC-77-Funkgeräte stellten die Verbindung zwischen den einzelnen Zügen und dem Kompaniekommando dar. Manche Einheiten trugen immer noch die kugelsichere M69-Weste. Zwei fluoreszierende Besätze am Helmband waren des Nachts für die Männer dahinter sichtbar. Siehe separat die Divisionsabzeichen.

E1 Diese Brigade wurde in normalen Stoffuniformen und Lederstiefeln nach Panama geschickt; die Soldaten sind besonders für das 'Tarnnest' auf den Helmen bekannt. Die große Gürteltasche enthält einen 200-schüssigen Patronengürtel für das leichte M249-Maschinengewehr; ein 30-schüssiges Magazin für das M16-Gewehr wird in einem kleineren Beutel mitgetragen und kann auch für das MG verwendet werden. Siehe separat die Divisionsabzeichen. E2 Heckenschützen trugen entweder M21- oder das neue M24-Gewehre. Ein reflektierender Streifen am Helm ist durch ein spezielles Nachtsichtgerät erkennbar, das sich an Bord von US-Flug-zeugen befindet, so daß die eigenen Truppen auch aus großer Höhe identifiziert werden können. Die alten M56- oder M61-Kampfranzen werden immer noch oft von der leichten Infanterie benutzt. E3 Luftwaffen-Bodentruppen koordinierten die Luftunterstützung. Zur normalen Ausrüstung gehörten Funkgerät AN/PRC-113-Funkgerät, Karabiner GAU-5, M9-Pistole, Signallampen usw. Armeeuniform mit USAF-Insignien wurde getragen. Siehe separat die Abzeichen

troupes pour coordonner l'assistance aérienne. L'équipement normal comprenait une radio AN/PRC-113, une carabine GAU-5, un pistolet M9, une lampe radar, etc. L'uniforme de l'Armée terrestre était porté avec l'insigne USAF. En cartouche, l'insigne TACW 602nd, porté sur la poche gauche; une partie du personnel portait également l'insigne de l'unité militaire qu'ils accompagnaient, sur la manche gauche. E4 Ces hommes portaient ce béret lorsqu'ils ne combattaient pas. Les officiers, contrairement aux grades subalternes, portaient un insigne supplémentaire de la 27th TASS à droite sur la poitrine.

F1 On sait peu de chose sur les uniformes de la Delta Force, hormis le fait qu'une grande latitude était permise; les combinaisons des équipages aériens avaient apparemment la préférence, de même que le camouflage BDU standard ou les vêtements noirs, et les coiffures étaient peu courantes. Le drapeau était le seul insigne porté. Il a une mitraillette silencieuse H & K et des lunettes protectrices pour la nuit. F2 BDU standard sans insigne sauf le drapeau, et un chapeau 'boonie'; fusil M16A2 et fusée anti-char M136. En cartouche, insigne des Forces Spéciales. F3 BDU léger, bottes de jungle et équipement ALICE; montre de plongée, boussole, et lunettes protectrices anti-laser; gants de pilote; et fusil M16A1 équipé d'un chargeur-tambour de 100 coups. En cartouche, insigne de guerre des Forces Marines spéciales.

G1 Uniforme et armes standard; hormis le brassard portant un insigne de formation ou l'écusson du drapeau, aucun insigne spécial MP n'était porté pendant les opérations. G2 Un autre policier militaire, ici avec une forme atténuée de l'insigne d'unité; l'insigne de brigade est aussi présenté en cartouche. G3 Un véhicule M1025 tel qu'il était utilisé par des équipes MP composées de trois hommes, avec mitrailleuse M60. Le ruban spécial visible de nuit était fixé aux coins du toit pour être repéré par les avions. G4 Personnel féminin en service dans les unités de soutien qui affrontent les dangers du combat dans les conditions modernes, certaines femmes durent ainsi utiliser leurs armes à Panama. Il n'y a pas de différence entre les uniformes de combat féminins et masculins.

H1 Seuls les Marines avaient en 1989 ce véhicule blindé de 17 tonnes, pour sept hommes, équipé d'un canon de 25 mm et de deux mitrailleuses; son succès fut tel que l'Armée des Etats-Unis commença à acheter les LAV-25. H2 Hormis le casque d'équipage de véhicule de combat DH132, il est habillé et équipé comme n'importe quel autre Marine US. H3 Membre d'une équipe spéciale anti-terroriste, portant un calot au lieu d'un casque pour avoir une meilleure vision et une meilleure ouïe lorsqu'il fouille des bâtiments; le ruban de reconnaissance spécial est posé sur le haut du calot. Toutes sortes d'armes sont utilisées par les forces spéciales; ce Marine porte une mitraillette Colt M16, et la carabine (en cartouche) Mossberg 590 est également populaire. H4 Le SMAW, une arme de conception israélienne, sert pour pénétrer de force les blockhaus et les bâtiments plutôt que contre des véhicules blindés. Ce Marine porte également le pistolet M9, une baïonnette/coupe-fils, et, comme tous les Marines, une trousse médicale de premier secours sur son ceinturon.

I Uniformes des Forces de Défense panaméennes. Ceux-ci étaient quasi-identiques aux BDU américains dans la plupart des cas, les soldats portaient également l'équipement ALICE, et même le casque 'Fritz' pour certaines unités d'élite, il était donc difficile de les distinguer pendant les combats. Des cartouchières fabriquées en Allemagne de l'Est furent distribuées à certaines unités équipées de fusils AK. Des uniformes de camouflage et vert olive furent portés, avec toute une variété de coiffure. I1 La 1st Infantry Company 'Tiger' était attachée au bataillon d'élite 2000 et avait donc des casques Kevlar. Il opère un fusil sans recul de 90 mm US M67. En cartouche, l'insigne de la compagnie. I2 La 2nd Infantry Airborne Company 'Puma' portait souvent les 'ailes' de parachutiste sur le béret à côté de l'insigne de la compagnie. Ce lieutenant déploie aussi son grade, le monogramme de nationalité 'RP', et l'insigne de l'École de Survie dans la Jungle, le monogramme de nationalité 'RP', et l'insigne des fusils croisés de l'infanterie. I3 L'insigne en cartouche se portait sur un béret marron pourpre en dehors des combats. Il porte un lance-roquettes soviétique RPG-7. I4 Ce bataillon (insigne en cartouche) portait un mélange de vêtements civils et militaires dans un rôle de semi-guérilla. Les armes sont un AK-47 et un mortier Soltam, israélien, de 60 mm.

J1 L'unité possédait en tout 13 véhicules blindés armés de mitrailleuse comme celui-ci, plus un peloton de soutien avec le V-300. J2 Ces voitures blindées, avec un canon de 90 mm, furent détruites sur le pont de la rivière Pacora par des troupes USSF et des avions de l'USAF pendant la seule tentative sérieuse du Bataillon d'Élite 2000 de résister contre l'invasion.

K1 Il y avait des hommes de plusieurs unités parmi les défenseurs du quartier général de Noriega. Ce caporal de la 6ème Compagnie mécanisée porte un MPiMS-72 fabriqué en Allemagne de l'Est; son insigne d'unité (voir J1) est imprimé sur son T-shirt. K2 Insigne de compagnie porté sur un béret de camouflage; pistolet à grenades de 40 mm, H&K, ouest-allemand et un fusil T-65. K3 Uniforme de caserne avec insigne de couleur de cette unité du Bataillon 2000; il porte un FN-MAG belge.

L1 Adjudant-chef d'un équipage d'hélicoptère en uniforme complet de vol. En cartouche, insigne de l'US Army South. L2 Pilote d'un OA-37B de l'Armée de l'Air en tenue contrastante de pilote de jet, avec gilet de sauvetage et veste de survie — voir les légendes en anglais pour les désignations des articles. L3 Canonnier d'un AC-130H Spectre de l'Air Force. La pelle est essentielle pour nettoyer les montagnes de cartouches qui jonchent le plancher du vaisseau lorsque ses canons sont en action. En cartouche, insigne d'escadron.

von 602. TACW, getragen auf der linken Tasche. Manche trugen auch das Abzeichen der Armee-Einheit, die sie begleiteten, am linken Ärmel. E4 Die Kappe wird nur getragen, wenn nicht im Einsatz. Die Offiziere trugen im Gegensatz zu niedrigeren Rängen noch das zusätzliche Abzeichen von der 27. TASS auf der rechten Brustseite.

F1 Über die Uniformen der Einheit Delta Force ist wenig bekannt, abgesehen davon, daß es dort größere Freiheiten gab; die Overalls der Flugzeugbesatzungen wurden offenbar bevorzugt, ebenso wie die normale BDU-Tarnuniform oder schwarze Uniformen; Kopfbedeckungen waren selten. Die Flagge wurde als einziges Abzeichen getragen. Er trägt eine H&K-Maschinenpistole mit Schalldämpfer sowie AN/PVS-7A-Nachtsichtbrillen. Siehe separat Abzeichen des Speziellen Einsatzkommandos der US-Armee. F2 Standard-BDU-Uniform ohne Abzeichen außer Flagge, und sog. 'Boonie'-Helm. M16A2-Gewehr und M136-Panzerabwehrrakete, Taucher-Armbanduhr, Kompaß und laserfeste Schutzbrillen; Pilotenhandschuhe und M16A1-Gewehr mit 100-schüssiger Magazintrommel. Separat siehe Naval Special Warfare-Abzeichen.

G1 Standard-Uniform und Bewaffnung; abgesehen von Umhängschild mit entweder Einheits-Abzeichen oder Flaggenabzeichen wurden im Dienst keine speziellen Militärpolizeiabzeichen getragen. G2 Ein anderer Militärpolizist, hier mit unauffälligerem Einheitsabzeichen; separat siehe Brigadeabzeichen. G3 M1025-Fahrzeug für drei-köpfige MP-Streifen, mit M60-Maschinengewehr. Das spezielle, des Nachts sichtbare Band wurde zwecks Identifizierung durch Flugzeuge am Dach des Fahrzeugs befestigt. G4 Weibliches Militärpersonal ist in Unterstützungseinheiten tätig, die bei der modernen Kriegführung auch unter Feuer geraten können; manche benutzten in Panama tatsächlich ihre Waffen. Es besteht kein Unterschied zwischen weiblichen und männlichen Kampfuniformen.

H1 1989 besaßen nur die Marineinfanteristen dieses gepanzerte, siebensitzige Fahrzeug mit 25 mm-Kanone und zwei MGs; der Erfolg war derart, daß ebenfalls der Ankauf dieser LAV-25-Fahrzeuge begonnen wurde. H2 Spezieller Anti-Terrorist-Kommandosoldat, mit Kappe anstatt Helm für bessere Sicht und besseres Hören beim Durchsuchen von Gebäuden; das spezielle Identifizierungsband wurde um die Kappe getragen. Diese speziellen Marine-Sondereinheiten tragen alle Arten von Waffen; dieser Mann trägt eine M16-Colt-Maschinenpistole; das separat gezeigte Gewehr Mossberg 590 ist ebenfalls beliebt. H4 Die von den Israelis entworfene SMAW-Angriffswaffe wird für das Eindringen in Bunker oder andere Gebäude eher benutzt als gegen Panzerfahrzeuge. Dieser Marineinfanterist trägt ferner eine M9-Pistole, eine Drahtschere/Bajonett und — wie alle seine Kameraden — einen Erste Hilfe-Beutel am Gürtel.

I Uniformen der panamanischen Verteidigungstruppen. Sie sind in den meisten Fällen fast identisch mit BDU-Uniformen, und da auch ALICE-Ausrüstung getragen wurde sowie bei manchen Elite-Einheiten auch der 'Fritz'-Helm, war die Identifizierung im Kampf recht schwierig. Manche mit AK-Gewehren ausgerüstete Einheiten hatten ostdeutsche Munitionsbeutel. Sowohl olivgrüne als auch Tarnuniformen wurden getragen, mit verschiedenen Helmen. I1 Die 1.Infanteriekompanie 'Tiger' gehörte zum Elite-Bataillon 2000, trug also Kevlar-Helme. Er trägt eine rückstoßfreie M67-90 mm-Büchse. Siehe separat Kompanieabzeichen. I2 Die 2. Fallschirmjägerkompanie 'Puma' trugen oft ihre Fallschirmjäger-Schwingen zusammen mit dem Kompanieabzeichen auf der Kappe. Dieser Leutnant zeigt auch seinen Rang und das Dschungel-Ausbildungsabzeichen, aufgestickte RP- und Infanterieabzeichen mit gekreuzten Gewehren. I3 Das separat gezeigte Abzeichen wurde auf einer braunen Kappe getragen, wenn nicht im Einsatz. Er trägt einen sowjetischen RPG-7-Raketenwerfer. I4 Dieses Bataillon (Abzeichen separat) trägt eine Mischung aus militärischen und zivilen Kleidungsstücken in seiner Semi-Guerillarolle. Die Waffen sind ein AK-47 und ein israelischer Soltam 60 mm-Mörser.

J1 Die Einheit besaß insgesamt 13 solche gepanzerten und mit MGs ausgerüstete Wagen, sowie eine Zusatztruppe mit der V-300. J2 Diese gepanzerten Wagen mit 90 mm-Kanonen wurden bei der Pacora-Brücke von USSF-Truppen und USAF-Flugzeugen bei dem einzigen ernsthaften Versuch des Elite-Bataillons 2000 vernichtet, der Invasion Widerstand zu leisten.

K1 Unter den Verteidigern des Hauptquartiers von Noriega befanden sich Angehörige verschiedener Einheiten. Dieser Obergefreite der 6. Mechanisierten Kompanie trägt eine ostdeutsche MPiMS-72; das Abzeichen dieser Einheit (siehe J1) sind auf das T-Shirt aufgedruckt. K2 Kompanieabzeichen auf der Tarnkappe; west-deutsche H&K 40mm-Granatenpistole und T-65-Gewehr. K3 Kasernen-uniform mit Farbabzeichen dieser Einheit von Bat. 2000; er trägt ein belgisches FN-MAG.

L1 Hubschrauber-Unteroffizier mit voller Fliegeruniform Siehe separat Abzeichen der US Army South. L2 Pilot eines Air Force OA-37B in kontrastierender Uniform eines Düsenjäger-Piloten, mit Schwimmweste und Notweste — siehe englischsprachige Bildtexte für nähere Beschreibung. L3 Schütze im schweren AC-130H Spectre-Hubschrauber der Air Force; die Schaufel ist wichtig, um den Berg von Patronen-hülsen fortzuschaffen, der den Boden des Hubschraubers bedeckt, wenn die Kanonen feuern. Siehe separat Staffelabzeichen.